Comptroller of the Currency
Administrator of National Banks

I0448207

# Asset Securitization

## Comptroller's Handbook

November 1997

L

# Asset Securitization
# Table of Contents

## Background

Asset securitization is helping to shape the future of traditional commercial banking.  By using the securities markets to fund portions of the loan portfolio, banks can allocate capital more efficiently, access diverse and cost-effective funding sources, and better manage business risks.

But securitization markets offer challenges as well as opportunity.   Indeed, the successes of nonbank securitizers are forcing banks to adopt some of their practices.  Competition from commercial paper underwriters and captive finance companies has taken a toll on banks' market share and profitability in the prime credit and consumer loan businesses.  And the growing competition within the banking industry from specialized firms that rely on securitization puts pressure on more traditional banks to use securitization to streamline as much of their credit and originations business as possible.  Because securitization may have such a fundamental impact on banks and the financial services industry, bankers and examiners should have a clear understanding of its benefits and inherent risks.

This booklet begins with an overview of the securitization markets, followed by a discussion of the mechanics of securitization.  The discussion evolves to the risks of securitization and how, at each stage of the process, banks are able to manage those risks.

A central theme of this booklet is the bank's use of asset securitization as a means of funding, managing the balance sheet, and generating fee income.  The discussion of risk focuses on banks' roles as financial intermediaries, that is, as loan originators and servicers rather than as investors in asset-backed securities.  Although purchasing asset-backed securities as investments clearly helps to diversify assets and manage credit quality, these benefits are discussed in other OCC publications, such as the "Investment Securities" section of the *Comptroller's Handbook.*

# Definition

Asset securitization is the structured process whereby interests in loans and other receivables are packaged, underwritten, and sold in the form of "asset-backed" securities. From the perspective of credit originators, this market enables them to transfer some of the risks of ownership to parties more willing or able to manage them. By doing so, originators can access the funding markets at debt ratings higher than their overall corporate ratings, which generally gives them access to broader funding sources at more favorable rates. By removing the assets and supporting debt from their balance sheets, they are able to save some of the costs of on-balance-sheet financing and manage potential asset-liability mismatches and credit concentrations.

# Brief History

Asset securitization began with the structured financing of mortgage pools in the 1970s. For decades before that, banks were essentially portfolio lenders; they held loans until they matured or were paid off. These loans were funded principally by deposits, and sometimes by debt, which was a direct obligation of the bank (rather than a claim on specific assets).

But after World War II, depository institutions simply could not keep pace with the rising demand for housing credit. Banks, as well as other financial intermediaries sensing a market opportunity, sought ways of increasing the sources of mortgage funding. To attract investors, investment bankers eventually developed an investment vehicle that isolated defined mortgage pools, segmented the credit risk, and structured the cash flows from the underlying loans. Although it took several years to develop efficient mortgage securitization structures, loan originators quickly realized the process was readily transferable to other types of loans as well.

Since the mid 1980s, better technology and more sophisticated investors have combined to make asset securitization one of the fastest growing activities in the capital markets. The growth rate of nearly every type of securitized asset has been remarkable, as have been the increase in the types of companies using securitization and the expansion of the investor base. The business of a credit intermediary has so changed that few banks, thrifts, or finance companies can afford to view themselves exclusively as portfolio lenders.

## Market Evolution

The market for mortgage-backed securities was boosted by the government agencies that stood behind these securities. To facilitate the securitization of nonmortgage assets, businesses substituted private credit enhancements. First, they overcollateralized pools of assets; shortly thereafter, they improved third-party and structural enhancements. In 1985, securitization techniques that had been developed in the mortgage market were applied for the first time to a class of nonmortgage assets — automobile loans. A pool of assets second only to mortgages, auto loans were a good match for structured finance; their maturities, considerably shorter than those of mortgages, made the timing of cash flows more predictable, and their long statistical histories of performance gave investors confidence.

The first significant bank credit card sale came to market in 1986 with a private placement of $50 million of bank card outstandings. This transaction demonstrated to investors that, if the yields were high enough, loan pools could support asset sales with higher expected losses and administrative costs than was true within the mortgage market. Sales of this type — with no contractual obligation by the seller to provide recourse — allowed banks to receive sales treatment for accounting and regulatory purposes (easing balance sheet and capital constraints), while at the same time allowing them to retain origination and servicing fees. After the success of this initial transaction, investors grew to accept credit card receivables as collateral, and banks developed structures to normalize the cash flows.

The next growth phase of securitization will likely involve nonconsumer assets. Most retail lending is readily "securitizable" because cash flows are predictable. Today, formula-driven credit scoring and credit monitoring techniques are widely used for such loans, and most retail programs produce fairly homogeneous loan portfolios. Commercial financing presents a greater challenge. Because a portfolio of commercial loans is typically less homogeneous than a retail portfolio, someone seeking to invest in them must often know much more about each individual credit, and the simpler tools for measuring and managing portfolio risk are less effective. Nonetheless, investment bankers and asset originators have proven extremely innovative at structuring cash flows and credit enhancements. Evidence of this can be seen in the market for securitized commercial real estate mortgages. Commercial real estate is one of the fastest-growing types of nonconsumer assets in the securitization markets, which fund approximately 10 percent of commercial mortgage debt.

## Benefits of Asset Securitization

The evolution of securitization is not surprising given the benefits that it offers to each of the major parties in the transaction.

### For Originators

Securitization improves returns on capital by converting an on-balance-sheet lending business into an off-balance-sheet fee income stream that is less capital intensive. Depending on the type of structure used, securitization may also lower borrowing costs, release additional capital for expansion or reinvestment purposes, and improve asset/liability and credit risk management.

### For Investors

Securitized assets offer a combination of attractive yields (compared with other instruments of similar quality), increasing secondary market liquidity, and generally more protection by way of collateral overages and/or guarantees by entities with high and stable credit ratings. They also offer a measure of flexibility because their payment streams can be structured to meet investors' particular requirements. Most important, structural credit enhancements and diversified asset pools free investors of the need to obtain a detailed understanding of the underlying loans. This has been the single largest factor in the growth of the structured finance market.

### For Borrowers

Borrowers benefit from the increasing availability of credit on terms that lenders may not have provided had they kept the loans on their balance sheets. For example, because a market exists for mortgage-backed securities, lenders can now extend fixed rate debt, which many consumers prefer over variable rate debt, without overexposing themselves to interest rate risk. Credit card lenders can originate very large loan pools for a diverse customer base at lower rates than if they had to fund the loans on their balance sheet. Nationwide competition among credit originators, coupled with strong investor appetite for the securities, has significantly expanded both the availability of credit and the pool of cardholders over the past decade.

Before evaluating how a bank manages the risks of securitization, an examiner should have a fundamental understanding of asset-backed securities and how they are structured. This section characterizes asset-backed securities, briefly discusses the roles of the major parties, and describes the mechanics of their cash flow, or how funds are distributed.

## Basic Structures of Asset-Backed Securities

A security's structure is often dictated by the kind of collateral supporting it. Installment loans dictate a quite different structure from revolving lines of credit. Installment loans, such as those made for the purchase of automobiles, trucks, recreational vehicles, and boats, have defined amortization schedules and fixed final maturity dates. Revolving loans, such as those extended to credit card holders and some home equity borrowers, have no specific amortization schedule or final maturity date. Revolving loans can be extended and repaid repeatedly over time, more or less at the discretion of the borrower.

### Installment Contract Asset-Backed Securities

Typical installment contract asset-backed securities, which bear a close structural resemblance to mortgage pass-through securities, provide investors with an undivided interest in a specific pool of assets owned by a trust. The trust is established by pooling installment loan contracts on automobiles, boats, or other assets purchased from a loan originator, often a bank.

The repayment terms for most installment contract asset-backed securities call for investors to receive a pro rata portion of all of the interest and principal received by the trust each month. Investors receive monthly interest on the outstanding balance of their certificates, including a full month's interest on any prepayments. The amount of principal included in each payment depends on the amortization and prepayment rate of the underlying collateral. Faster prepayments shorten the average life of the issue.

**Revolving Asset Transactions**

The typically short lives of receivables associated with revolving loan products (credit cards, home equity lines, etc.) require issuers to modify the structures used to securitize the assets. For example, a static portfolio of credit card receivables typically has a life of between five months and ten months. Because such a life is far too short for efficient security issuance, securities backed by revolving loans are structured in a manner to facilitate management of the cash flows. Rather than distributing principal and interest to investors as received, the securities distribute cash flow in stages — a revolving phase followed by an amortization phase. During the revolving period, only interest is paid and principal payments are reinvested in additional receivables as, for example, customers use their credit cards or take additional draws on their home equity lines. At the end of the revolving period an amortization phase begins, and principal payments are made to investors along with interest payments. Because the principal balances are repaid over a short time, the life of the security is largely determined by the length of the revolving period.

## Parties to the Transaction

The securitization process redistributes risk by breaking up the traditional role of a bank into a number of specialized roles: originator, servicer, credit enhancer, underwriter, trustee, and investor. Banks may be involved in several of the roles and often specialize in a particular role or roles to take advantage of expertise or economies of scale. The types and levels of risk to which a particular bank is exposed will depend on the organization's role in the securitization process.

With sufficient controls and the necessary infrastructure in place, securitization offers several advantages over the traditional bank lending model. These benefits, which may increase the soundness and efficiency of the credit extension process, can include a more efficient origination process, better risk diversification, and improved liquidity. A look at the roles played by the primary participants in the securitization process will help to illustrate the benefits.

**Exhibit 1: Parties Involved in Structuring Asset-Backed Securities**

```
                          ┌──────────────┐
                          │   Borrower   │
                          └──────┬───────┘
                                 │
                          ┌──────┴───────┐
                          │ Originator / │
                          │   Servicer   │
                          └──────┬───────┘
                                 │
  ┌──────────────┐        ┌──────┴───────┐        ┌──────────────┐
  │   Rating     │────────│   Special    │────────│    Credit    │
  │   Agency     │        │   Purpose    │        │   Enhancer   │
  └──────────────┘        │Entity/Trustee│        └──────────────┘
                          └──────┬───────┘
                                 │
                          ┌──────┴───────┐
                          │ Underwriter  │
                          └──────┬───────┘
                                 │
                          ┌──────┴───────┐
                          │  Investors   │
                          └──────────────┘
```

*Borrower.*  The borrower is responsible for payment on the underlying loans and therefore the ultimate performance of the asset-backed security.  Because borrowers often do not realize that their loans have been sold, the originating bank is often able to maintain the customer relationship.

From a credit risk perspective, securitization has made popular the practice of grouping borrowers by letter or categories.  At the top of the rating scale, 'A'-quality borrowers have relatively pristine credit histories.  At the bottom, 'D'-quality borrowers usually have severely blemished credit histories.  The categories are by no means rigid; in fact, credit evaluation problems exist because one originator's 'A' borrower may be another's 'A-' or 'B' borrower.  Nevertheless, the terms 'A' paper and 'B/C' paper are becoming more and more popular.

Exhibit 2 is an example of generic borrower descriptions used by Duff and Phelps Credit Rating Corporation in rating mortgage borrowers.  The borrowers' characteristics in the exhibit are generalizations of each category's standards and fluctuate over time; however, the table does provide an illustration of general standards in use today.  For example, an 'A' quality

**Exhibit 2: Borrower Credit Quality Categories**

| Generic Borrower Credit Quality Description | Mortgage Credit | Other Credit | Recency of Bankruptcy | Debt to Income Ratio | Loan-to-Value Guidelines |
|---|---|---|---|---|---|
| A: Standard agency quality | 1 x 30 last 12 months | No derogatories | 5 yrs. | 36% | 97% |
| A-: Very minor credit problems | 1 x 30 last 12 months 2 x 30 last 24 months | Minor derogatories explained | 5 yrs. | 42% | 90% |
| B: Minor to moderate credit problems | 4 x 30 last 12 months 1 x 60 last 24 months | Some prior defaults | 3 yrs. | 50% | 75% |
| C: Moderate to serious credit problems | 6 x 30 last 12 months 1 x 60 & 1 x 90 last 12 months | Significant credit problems | 18 months | 55% | 70% |
| D: Demonstrated unwillingness or inability to pay | 30-60 constant delinquent, 2 x 90 last 12 months | Severe credit problems | 12 months | 60% | 65% |

*(Source: Duff & Phelps)*

borrower will typically have an extensive credit history with few if any delinquencies, and a fairly strong capacity to service debt. In contrast, a 'C' quality borrower has a poor or limited credit history, numerous instances of delinquency, and may even have had a fairly recent bankruptcy. Segmenting borrowers by grade allows outside parties such as rating agencies to compare performance of a specific company or underwriter more readily with that of its peer group.

*Originator.* Originators create and often service the assets that are sold or used as collateral for asset-backed securities. Originators include captive finance companies of the major auto makers, other finance companies, commercial banks, thrift institutions, computer companies, airlines, manufacturers, insurance companies, and securities firms. The auto finance companies dominate the securitization market for automobile loans. Thrifts securitize primarily residential mortgages through pass-throughs, pay-throughs, or mortgage-backed bonds. Commercial banks regularly originate and securitize auto loans, credit card receivables, trade receivables, mortgage loans, and more recently small business loans. Computer companies, airlines, and other commercial companies often use securitization to finance receivables generated from sales of their primary products in the normal course of business.

*Servicer.* The originator/lender of a pool of securitized assets usually continues to service the securitized portfolio. (The only assets with an active secondary market for servicing contracts are mortgages.) Servicing includes customer service and payment processing for the borrowers in the securitized pool and collection actions in accordance with the pooling and servicing agreement. Servicing can also include default management and collateral liquidation. The servicer is typically compensated with a fixed normal servicing fee.

Servicing a securitized portfolio also includes providing administrative support for the benefit of the trustee (who is duty-bound to protect the interests of the investors). For example, a servicer prepares monthly informational reports, remits collections of payments to the trust, and provides the trustee with monthly instructions for the disposition of the trust's assets. Servicing reports are usually prepared monthly, with specific format requirements for each performance and administrative report. Reports are distributed to the investors, the trustee, the rating agencies, and the credit enhancer.

*Trustee.* The trustee is a third party retained for a fee to administer the trust that holds the underlying assets supporting an asset-backed security. Acting in a fiduciary capacity, the trustee is primarily concerned with preserving the rights of the investor. The responsibilities of the trustee will vary from issue to issue and are delineated in a separate trust agreement. Generally, the trustee oversees the disbursement of cash flows as prescribed by the indenture or pooling and servicing agreement, and monitors compliance with appropriate covenants by other parties to the agreement.

If problems develop in the transaction, the trustee focuses particular attention on the obligations and performance of all parties associated with the security, particularly the servicer and the credit enhancer. Throughout the life of the transaction the trustee receives periodic financial information from the originator/servicer delineating amounts collected, amounts charged off, collateral values, etc. The trustee is responsible for reviewing this information to ensure that the underlying assets produce adequate cash flow to service the securities. The trustee also is responsible for declaring an event of default or an amortization event, as well as replacing the servicer if it fails to perform in accordance with the required terms.

*Credit Enhancer.* Credit enhancement is a method of protecting investors in the event that cash flows from the underlying assets are insufficient to pay the interest and principal due for the security in a timely manner. Credit enhancement is used to improve the credit rating, and therefore the pricing and marketability of the security.

As a general rule, third-party credit enhancers must have a credit rating at least as high as the rating sought for the security. Third-party credit support is often provided through a letter of credit or surety bond from a highly rated bank or insurance company. Because there are currently few available highly rated third-party credit enhancers, internal enhancements such as the senior/subordinated structure have become popular for many asset-backed deals. In this latter structure, the assets themselves and cash collateral accounts provide the credit support. These cash collateral accounts and separate, junior classes of securities protect the senior classes by absorbing defaults before the senior position's cash flows are interrupted.

*Rating Agencies.* The rating agencies perform a critical role in structured finance — evaluating the credit quality of the transactions. Such agencies are considered credible because they possess the expertise to evaluate various underlying asset types, and because they do not have a financial interest in a security's cost or yield. Ratings are important because investors generally accept ratings by the major public rating agencies in lieu of conducting a due diligence investigation of the underlying assets and the servicer.

Most nonmortgage asset-backed securities are rated. The large public issues are rated because the investment policies of many corporate investors require ratings. Private placements are typically rated because insurance companies are a significant investor group, and they use ratings to assess capital reserves against their investments. Many regulated investors, such as life insurance companies, pension funds, and to some extent commercial banks can purchase only limited amounts of securities rated below investment grade.

The rating agencies review four major areas:

- Quality of the assets being sold,
- Abilities and strength of the originator/servicer of the assets,

- Soundness of the transaction's overall structure, and
- Quality of the credit support.

From this review, the agencies assess the likelihood that the security will pay interest and principal according to the terms of the trust agreement. The rating agencies focus solely on the credit risk of an asset-backed security. They do not express an opinion on market value risks arising from interest rate fluctuations or prepayments, or on the suitability of an investment for a particular investor.

*Underwriter.* The asset-backed securities underwriter is responsible for advising the seller on how to structure the security, and for pricing and marketing it to investors. Underwriters are often selected because of their relationships with institutional investors and for their advice on the terms and pricing required by the market. They are also generally familiar with the legal and structural requirements of regulated institutional investors.

*Investors.* The largest purchasers of securitized assets are typically pension funds, insurance companies, fund managers, and, to a lesser degree, commercial banks. The most compelling reason for investing in asset-backed securities has been their high rate of return relative to other assets of comparable credit risk. The OCC's investment securities regulations at 12 CFR 1 allow national banks to invest up to 25 percent of their capital in "Type V" securities. By definition, a Type V security:

- Is marketable,
- Is rated investment grade,
- Is fully secured by interests in a pool of loans to numerous obligors and in which a national bank could invest directly, and
- Is not rated as a mortgage-related or Type IV security.

## Structuring the Transaction

The primary difference between whole loan sales or participations and securitized credit pools is the structuring process. Before most loan pools can be converted into securities, they must be structured to modify the nature of the risks and returns to the final investors. Structuring includes the isolation and distribution of credit risk, usually through credit enhancement techniques, and the use of trusts and special purpose entities to address tax issues and the management of cash flows.

Examiners performing a comprehensive review of a specific securitization process should read through the pooling and servicing agreement and/or a specific series supplement for explicit detail on the structure and design of the particular asset-backed security and the responsibilities of each involved party. For purposes of this booklet, the following is an overview of the structuring process and a description of what the documents usually contain.

Generally, the structure of a transaction is governed by the terms of the pooling and servicing agreement and, for master trusts, each series supplement. The pooling and servicing agreement is the primary contractual document between the seller/servicer and the trustee. This agreement documents the terms of the sale and the responsibilities of the seller/servicer. For master trusts, the pooling and servicing agreement, including the related series supplement, document the terms of the sale and responsibilities of the seller/servicer for a specific issuance. The following section describes the four major stages of the structuring process:

- Segregating the assets from the seller/originator.
- Creating a special-purpose vehicle to hold the assets and protect the various parties' interests.
- Adding credit enhancement to improve salability.
- Issuing interests in the asset pool.

## Segregating the Assets

Securitization allows investors to evaluate the quality of a security on its own (apart from the credit quality of the originator/seller). To accomplish this, the seller conveys receivables to a trust for the benefit of certificate holders. For revolving-type assets, this conveyance includes the amount of receivables in certain designated accounts on a specific cutoff date, plus the option for the trust to purchase any new receivables that arise from those designated accounts subsequent to the cutoff date. The accounts and receivables are subject to eligibility criteria and specific representations and warranties of the seller.

## Choosing Accounts — Initial Pool Selection

The seller designates which accounts' receivables will be sold to a trust. The selection is carried out with an eye to creating a portfolio whose performance is not only predictable but also consistent with the target quality of the desired security. Step one is determining which accounts will be "designated" as those from which receivables may be included in the trust. For example, past-due receivables may be left in the eligible pool, but accounts that have had a default or write-off may be excluded. Some issuers include written-off receivables, allowing the revenue from recoveries to become part of the cash flow of the trust. Other selection criteria might include data elements such as geographic location, maturity date, size of the credit line, or age of the account relationship.

Step two, asset selection, can either be random, in order to create selections that are representative of the total portfolio, or inclusive, so that all qualifying receivables are sold. In random selection, the issuer determines how many accounts are needed to meet the target value of the security; then the accounts are selected randomly (for example, every sixth account is selected from the eligible universe).

## Account Additions and Removals

For trusts with a revolving feature, such as credit cards or home equity lines of credit, the seller may be required to designate additional accounts that will be assimilated by the trust. This may be required for a variety of reasons, for example, when the seller's interest (the interest in the receivables pool retained by the seller subsequent to transfer into the trust) falls below a level specified in the pooling and servicing agreement. The seller also typically reserves the ability to withdraw some accounts previously designated for the trust.[1] Rating agencies must often be notified when account additions or removals reach certain thresholds. For example, the terms of the rating may

---

[1] The issue of whether provisions for the removal of accounts are in-substance call options retained by the seller (which may compromise sales treatment) is under consideration by FASB at the time of this writing. A formal FASB interpretation is expected to be issued in exposure draft form. Until then, the guidance under Emerging Issues Task Force (EITF) Issue 90-18 remains in effect.

require rating agency confirmation that account additions or removals do not lower outstanding ratings when additions or removals exceed 15 percent of the balance at the beginning of the previous quarter.

## Creating Securitization Vehicles

Banks usually structure asset-backed securities using "grantor trusts," "owner trusts," or other "revolving asset trusts," each of which customarily issues different types of securities. In choosing a trust structure, banks seek to ensure that the transaction insulates the assets from the reach of the issuer's creditors and that the issuer, securitization vehicle, and investors receive favorable tax treatment.

In a *grantor trust*, the certificate holders (investors) are treated as beneficial owners of the assets sold. The net income from the trust is taxed on a pass-through basis as if the certificate holders directly owned the receivables. To qualify as a grantor trust, the structure of the deal must be passive — that is, the trust cannot engage in profitable activities for the investors, and there cannot be "multiple classes" of interest. Grantor trusts are commonly used when the underlying assets are installment loans whose interest and principal payments are reasonably predictable and fit the desired security structure.

In an *owner trust*, the assets are usually subject to a lien of indenture through which notes are issued. The beneficial ownership of the owner trust's assets (subject to the lien) is represented by certificates, which may be sold or retained by the bank. An owner trust, properly structured, will be treated as a partnership under the Internal Revenue Code of 1986. A partnership, like a grantor trust, is effectively a pass-through entity under the Internal Revenue Code and therefore does not pay federal income tax. Instead, each certificate holder (including the special-purpose corporation) must separately take into account its allocated share of income, gains, losses, deductions, and credits of the trust. Like the grantor trust, the owner trust is expressly limited in its activities by its charter, although owner trusts are typically used when the cash flows of the assets must be "managed" to create "bond-like" securities. Unlike a grantor trust, the owner trust can issue securities in multiple series with different maturities, interest rates, and cash flow priorities.

*Revolving asset trusts* may be either stand-alone or master trust structures. The stand-alone trust is simply a single group of accounts whose receivables are sold to a trust and used as collateral for a single security, although there may be several classes within that security. When the issuer intends to issue another security, it simply designates a new group of accounts and sells their receivables to a separate trust. As the desire for additional flexibility, efficiency, and uniformity of collateral performance for various series issued by the same originator has increased over time, the stand-alone structure evolved into the master trust structure.

Master trusts allow an issuer to sell a number of securities (and series) at different times from the same trust. All of the securities rely on the same pool of receivables as collateral. In a master trust, each certificate of each series represents an undivided interest in all of the receivables in the trust. This structure provides the issuer with much more flexibility, since issuing a new series from a master trust costs less and requires less effort than creating a new trust for every issue. In addition, credit evaluation of each series in a master trust is much easier since the pool of receivables will be larger and less susceptible to seasonal or demographic concentrations. Credit cards, home equity lines of credit, and other revolving assets are usually best packaged in these structures. A revolving asset trust is treated as a "security arrangement" and is ignored for tax purposes. (See following discussion under "Tax Issues.")

## Legal Issues

When banks are sellers of assets, they have two primary legal concerns. They seek to ensure that:

- A security interest in the assets securitized is perfected.
- The security is structured so as to preclude the FDIC's voiding of the perfected security interest.

By perfecting security interests, a lender protects the trustee's property rights from third parties who may have retained rights that impair the timely payment of debt service on the securities. Typically, a trustee requires a legal opinion to the effect that the trust has a first-priority perfected security interest in the pledged receivables. In general, filing Uniform Commercial Code documents (UCC-1) is sufficient for unsecured consumer loan receivables such as credit cards. For other types of receivables whose collateral is a reliable fall-back repayment source (such as automobile loans and home equity lines of credit), additional steps may be required (title amendments, mortgage liens, etc.) to perfect the trustee's security interest in the receivables and the underlying collateral.

If the seller/originator is a bank, the provisions of the U.S. Bankruptcy Code (11 USC 1 *et seq.*) do not apply to its insolvency proceedings. In the case of a bank insolvency, the FDIC would act as receiver or conservator of the financial institution.[2] Although the Federal Deposit Insurance Act does not contain an automatic stay provision that would stop the payout of securities (as does the bankruptcy code), the FDIC has the power to ask for a judicial stay of all payments or the repudiation of any contract. In order to avoid inhibiting securitization, however, the FDIC has stated[3] that it would not seek to void an otherwise legally enforceable and perfected security interest provided:

- The agreement was undertaken in the ordinary course of business, not in contemplation of insolvency, and with no intent to hinder, delay, or defraud the bank or its creditors;
- The secured obligation represents a bona fide and arm's length transaction;
- The secured party or parties are not insiders or affiliates of the bank;
- The grant of the security interest was made for adequate consideration; and
- The security agreement evidencing the security interest is in writing, was duly approved by the board of directors of the bank or its loan committee, and remains an official record of the bank.

---

[2]  A national bank may not be a "debtor" under the bankruptcy code. *See* USC 109(b)(2). The FDIC may act as receiver or conservator of a failed institution, subject to appointment by the appropriate federal banking agency. *See* 12 USC 1821.

[3]  "Statement of Policy regarding Treatment of Security Interests after Appointment of the FDIC as Conservator or Receiver." March 31, 1993, 58 FR 16833.

## Tax Issues

Issuers ordinarily choose a structure that will minimize the impact of taxes on the security. Federal income tax can be minimized in two principal ways — by choosing a vehicle that is not subject to tax or by having the vehicle issue "debt" the interest on which is tax deductible (for the vehicle or its owners).

In a grantor trust, each certificate holder is treated as the owner of a pro rata share of the trust's assets and the trust is ignored for tax purposes. To receive the favorable tax treatment, each month the grantor trust must distribute all principal and interest received on the assets held by the trust. A grantor trust is not an "entity" for federal tax purposes; rather, its beneficiaries are treated as holders of a ratable share of its assets (in contrast to partnerships, which are treated as entities, even though their income is allocated to the holders of the partnership interests). The requirement that the trust be "passive" generally makes the grantor trust best suited for longer-term assets such as mortgages or automobile receivables.

An owner trust generally qualifies as a partnership for tax purposes. Because the issuer usually retains an interest in the assets or a reserve account, it is usually a partner; if so, the transfer of assets to the trust is governed by tax provisions on transfers to partnerships. Although the partnership itself would generally not be subject to tax, its income (net of deductions for interest paid to note holders) would be reportable by the partner certificate holders and the issuer. Partnership owner trusts are commonly used in fixed pool transactions involving the same kinds of assets that are securitized through grantor trusts; assets in owner trusts typically require more management or will be issued as more than one class of security.

The cash flows for shorter-term assets, such as credit cards, require too much management for a grantor trust. Although owner trusts are theoretically the appropriate vehicle for issuing such assets, in practice revolving asset trusts are usually used when the parties structure the transaction *for tax purposes* as a secured loan from the investors to the seller of the receivables. The trust is simply a means of securing financing and is ignored for tax purposes. (Such treatment — as a "security arrangement" — is like that accorded a grantor trust, which is also ignored for tax purposes, except that a grantor trust must file a tax report and a "security arrangement" does not.)

Assets requiring managed cash flows can also be structured as a special-purpose corporation (SPC), in which the asset-backed securities are debt of the issuer rather than ownership interests in the receivables. In this structure an SPC typically owns the receivables and sells debt that is backed by the assets, thus allowing the SPC to restructure the cash flows from the receivables into several debt tranches with varying maturities. The interest income from the receivables is taxable to the corporation, and this taxable income is largely offset by the tax deduction from the interest expense on the debt it issues.

Other securitization vehicles, such as real estate mortgage investment conduits (REMICs) and, more recently (effective September 1, 1997), financial asset securitization investment trusts (FASITs), are essentially statutory structures modeled after the "common law" structures described in the foregoing examples. In any event, the overriding objective remains the same: to receive the equivalent of "flow-through" treatment that minimizes the tax consequences for the cash flows. Because interpretations concerning tax treatment may change as structures evolve, banks are encouraged to consult with tax counsel on taxation issues arising from securitization.

## Providing Credit Enhancement

Securitization typically splits the credit risk into several tranches, placing it with parties that are willing or best able to absorb it. The first loss tranche is usually capped at levels approximate to the "expected" or "normal" rate of portfolio credit loss. All credit losses up to this point are effectively absorbed by the credit originator, since it typically receives portfolio cash flow after expenses (which include expected losses) in the form of excess spread.

The second tranche typically covers losses that exceed the originator's cap. This second level of exposure is usually capped at some multiple of the pool's expected losses (customarily between three times and five times these losses), depending on the desired credit ratings for the senior positions. This risk is often absorbed by a high-grade, well-capitalized credit enhancer that is able to diversify the risk (exhibit 3). The third tranche of credit risk is

**Exhibit 3: Credit risk diversification**

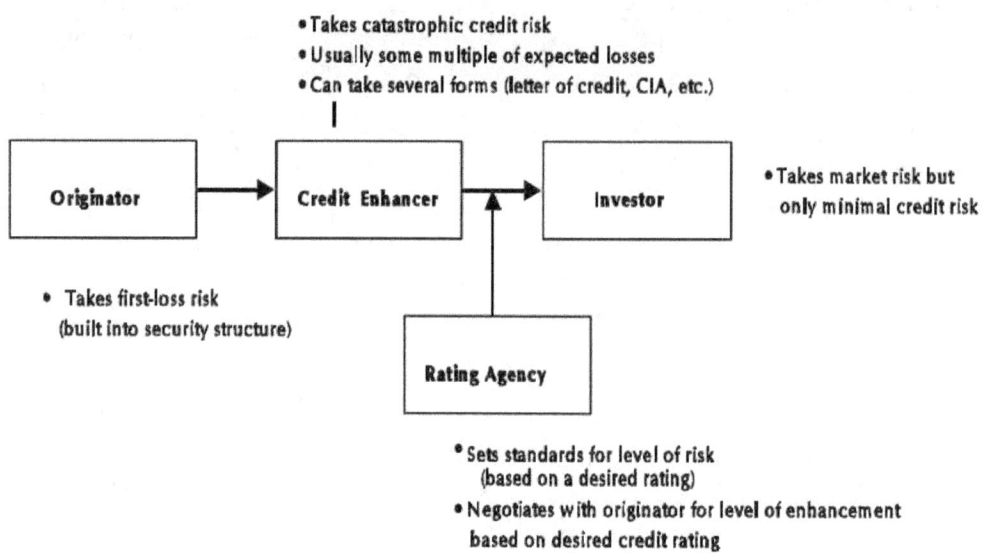

- Takes catastrophic credit risk
- Usually some multiple of expected losses
- Can take several forms (letter of credit, CIA, etc.)

| Originator | → | Credit Enhancer | → | Investor |

- Takes market risk but only minimal credit risk

- Takes first-loss risk (built into security structure)

**Rating Agency**

- Sets standards for level of risk (based on a desired rating)
- Negotiates with originator for level of enhancement based on desired credit rating

undertaken by the investors that buy the asset-backed securities themselves. Although investors are exposed to other types of risk, such as prepayment or interest rate risk, senior-level classes of asset-backed securities typically have little exposure to credit loss.

Aside from the coupon rate paid to investors, the largest expense in structuring an asset-backed security is the cost of credit enhancement. Issuers are constantly attempting to minimize the costs associated with providing credit protection to the ultimate investors. Credit enhancement comes in several different forms, although it can generally be divided into two main types: external (third-party or seller's guarantee) or internal (structural or cash-flow-driven). Common types of credit enhancements in use today include:

**Credit Enhancement Provided by External Parties**

- *Third-party letter of credit.* For issuers with credit ratings below the level sought for the security issued, a third party may provide a letter of credit to cover a certain amount of loss or percentage of losses. Draws on the letter of credit protection are often repaid (if possible) from excess cash flows from the securitized portfolio.

- *Recourse to seller.* Principally used by nonbank issuers, this method uses a limited guaranty of the seller covering a specified maximum amount of losses on the pool.

- *Surety bonds.* Guarantees issued by third parties, usually AAA-rated mono-line insurance companies. Surety bond providers generally guarantee (or wrap) the principal and interest payments of 100 percent of a transaction.

Although the ratings of third-party credit enhancers are rarely lowered, such an event could lower the rating of a security. As a result, issuers are relying less and less on third-party enhancement.

## Credit Enhancement Provided by Internal Structure

Structural features can be created to raise the credit quality of an asset-backed security. For example, a highly rated senior class of securities can be supported by one or more subordinate security classes and a cash collateral account. Senior/subordinate structures are layered so that each position benefits from the credit protection of all the positions subordinate to it. The junior positions are subordinate in the payment of both principal and interest to the senior positions in the securities.

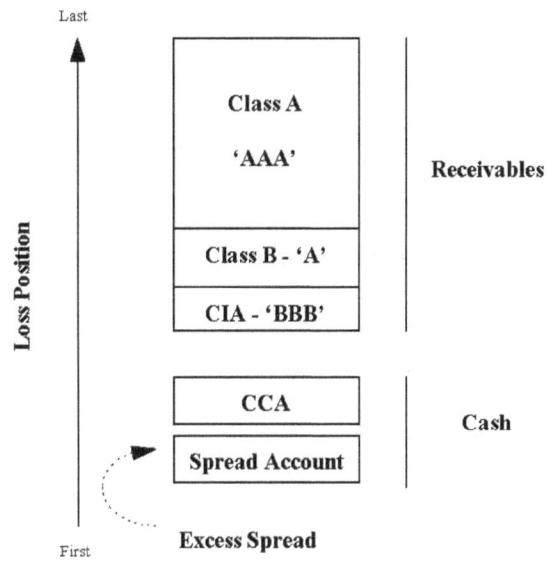

A typical security structure may contain any of the following internal enhancements (which are presented in order from junior to senior, that is, from the first to absorb losses to the last):

1. *Excess spread.* The portfolio yield for a given month on the receivables supporting an asset-backed security is generally greater than the

coupon, servicing costs, and expected losses for the issued securities. Any remaining finance charges after funding, servicing costs, and losses is called "excess spread." (See the cash flow waterfall discussion in the "Mechanics of Cash Flow" section, which follows, for an illustration of how excess spread is determined.) This *residual* amount normally reverts to the seller as additional profit. However, it is also commonly available to the trust to cover unexpected losses.

2. *Spread account.* Monthly finance charges from the underlying pool of receivables are available to cover unexpected losses in any given month. If not needed, this "excess spread" generally reverts to the seller. Many trusts provide that, if portfolio yield declines or losses increase, the monthly excess spread is captured, or "trapped," in a spread account (a form of cash collateral account) to provide future credit enhancement.

3. *Cash collateral accounts.* A cash collateral account is a segregated trust account, funded at the outset of the deal, that can be drawn on to cover shortfalls in interest, principal, or servicing expense for a particular series if excess spread is reduced to zero. The account can be funded by the issuer, but is often funded by a loan from a third-party bank, which will be repaid only after holders of all classes of certificates of that series have been repaid in full.

4. *Collateral invested amount (CIA).* The CIA is an uncertificated, privately placed ownership interest in the trust, subordinate in payment rights to all investor certificates. Like a layer of subordination, the CIA serves the same purpose as a cash collateral account: it makes up for shortfalls if excess spread is negative. The CIA is itself often protected by a cash collateral account and available monthly excess spread. If the CIA absorbs losses, it can be reimbursed from future excess spread if available.

5. *Subordinate security classes.* Subordinate classes are junior in claim to other debt — that is, they are repayable only after other classes of the security with a higher claim have been satisfied. Some securities contain more than one class of subordinate debt, and one subordinate class may have a higher claim than other such positions.

Most structures contain a combination of one or more of the enhancement techniques described above. For example, some issuers combine surety bond protection with senior/subordinate structures, creating "super senior" classes that are insulated from third-party risk and have higher rated subordinated classes because of the credit-wrap. The objective from an issuer's viewpoint is to find the most practical and cost-effective method of providing the credit protection necessary for the desired credit rating and pricing of the security.

Most securities also contain performance-related features designed to protect investors (and credit enhancers) against portfolio deterioration. These "performance triggers" are designed to increase the spread account available to absorb losses, to accelerate repayment of principal before pool performance would likely result in losses to investors, or both. The first (most sensitive) triggers typically capture excess spread within the trust (either additions to existing spread accounts or a separate reserve fund) to provide additional credit protection when a portfolio begins to show signs of deterioration. If delinquencies and loss levels continue to deteriorate, early amortization events may occur. Early amortization triggers are usually based on a three-month rolling average to ensure that amortization is accelerated only when performance is consistently weak.

The originator or pool sponsor will often negotiate with the rating agencies about the type and size of the internal and external credit enhancement. The size of the enhancement is dictated by the credit rating desired. For the highest triple-A rating, the rating agencies are likely to insist that the level of protection be sufficient to shield cash flows against circumstances as severe as those experienced during the Great Depression of the 1930s.

## Issuing Interests in the Asset Pool

On the closing date of the transaction, the receivables are transferred, directly or indirectly, from the seller to the special-purpose vehicle (trust). The trust issues certificates representing beneficial interests in the trust, investor certificates, and, in the case of revolving asset structures, a transferor (seller) certificate.

## Investors' Certificate

The investor certificates are sold in either public offerings or private placements, and the proceeds, net of issuance expenses, are remitted to the seller. There are two main types of investor interests in securitized assets — a discrete interest in *specific* assets and an undivided interest in a *pool* of assets. The first type of ownership interest is used for asset pools that match the maturity and cash flow characteristics of the security issued. The second type of interest is used for relatively short-term assets such as credit card receivables or advances against home equity lines of credit. For the shorter-term assets, new receivables are generated and added to the pool as the receivables liquidate, and the investor's undivided interest automatically applies to the new receivables in the pool.

## Seller's Interest

When receivables backing securities are short-term or turn over rapidly, as do trade receivables or credit cards, the cash flows associated with the receivables must be actively managed. One objective is to keep the outstanding principal balance of the investor's interest equal to the certificate amounts. To facilitate this equalization, an interest in trust structures, known as the "seller's" or "transferor's" interest, is not allocated to investors. The seller's interest serves two primary purposes: to provide a cash-flow buffer when account payments fall short of account purchases and to absorb reductions in the receivable balance attributable to dilution and noncomplying receivables.

To calculate the size of the seller's interest, subtract the amount of securities issued by the trust (liabilities) from the balance of principal receivables in the trust (assets). The seller's interest is generally not a form of credit enhancement for the investor interests.

# The Mechanics of Cash Flow

## Cash Flow Allocations

### Pass-Through Securities

The payment distribution for securities backed by installment loans is closely tied to the loans' payment flows. Interest is customarily paid monthly, and the principal included in each payment will depend on the amortization schedule and prepayment rate of the underlying collateral.

### Pay-Through Securities

For revolving asset types such as credit cards, trade receivables, and home equity lines, the cash flow has two phases:

- The revolving period; and
- The principal pay-down period (amortization phase).

During the revolving period, investors receive their pro rata share of the gross portfolio yield (see below) based on the principal amount of their certificates and the coupon rate. The remaining portion of their share of the finance charges above the coupon rate is available to pay the servicing fees and to cover any charge-offs, with residual amounts generally retained by the seller or credit enhancement provider as excess spread. This distribution of cash is often referred to as the "cash flow waterfall."

The cash flow waterfall for credit card securities may look like this (percentages based on investor's pro rata share of outstanding receivables):

*Revenue*

| | |
|---|---|
| Finance Charges | 16.5%* |
| Annual Fees | 1.5% |
| Late Fees and Other Fees | 0.7% |
| Interchange | 1.8% |
| **Gross Portfolio Yield (finance charges)** | **20.5%** |

*Expenses*

| | |
|---|---|
| Investor Coupon | 7.0%* |
| Servicing Expense | 2.5% |
| Charge-offs | 5.0% |
| **Total Expenses** | **14.5%** |
| **Excess Spread** | **6.0%** |

During the revolving period, monthly principal collections are used to purchase new receivables generated in the designated accounts or to purchase a portion of the seller's participation if there are no new receivables. If the percentage of the seller's interest falls below a prescribed level of principal outstanding because of a lack of new borrowings from the designated accounts, new accounts may be added.

After this revolving period comes the amortization period. During this phase, the investors' share of principal collections are no longer used to purchase replacement receivables. These proceeds are returned to investors as received. This is the simplest form of principal repayment. However, because over time investors have preferred more stable returns of principal, some issuers have created structures to accumulate principal payments in a trust account ("accumulation account") rather than simply passing principal payments through to investors as received. The trust then pays principal on a specific, or "bullet," maturity date. Bullet maturities are typically either "hard" or "soft," depending on how the structure compensates when funds in the accumulation account are not sufficient to pay investors in full on the scheduled maturity date. Under a hard bullet structure, a third-party maturity guaranty covers the shortfall. Under a soft bullet structure, the entire accumulation account is distributed to the investors and further funds are paid as received. Soft bullet structures usually include an expected maturity date and a final maturity date.

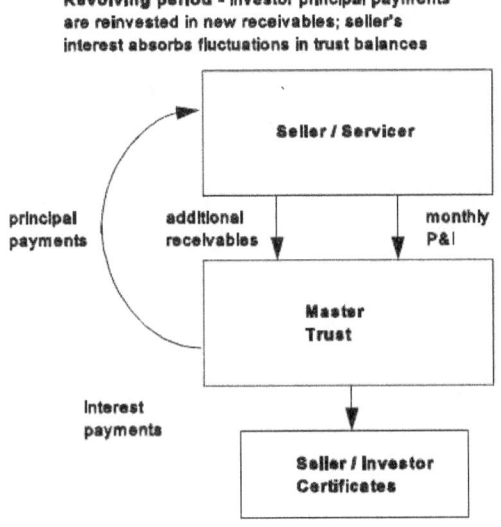

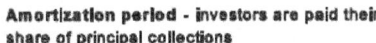

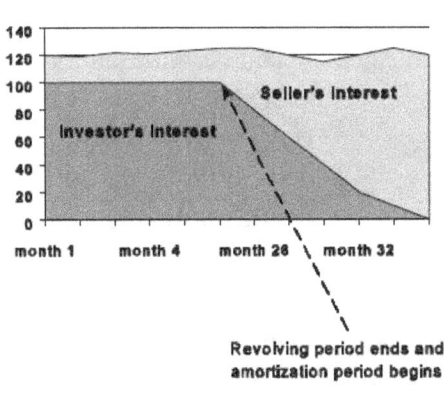

## Early Amortization Protection

In addition to the previously discussed credit enhancement types, revolving asset-backed securities typically use early amortization triggers to protect investors from credit risk. These triggers, or payout events, accelerate the repayment of investor principal if cash flow from the pool declines or the condition of the pooled assets deteriorates. This accelerated repayment method requires that the investors' share of all principal collections be returned immediately as it is received by the trust. The payout events are defined in the pooling and servicing agreement and series supplement of each securitization, and are intended to protect investors from prolonged exposure to deteriorating performance of the underlying assets or the default of a servicer.

To monitor the asset-backed security's performance, the trustee, the rating agencies, and investors focus on several indicators of pool performance: portfolio yield, the loss rate, the monthly payment rate, and the purchase rate.

- *Portfolio yield* generally consists of three types of payments: finance charges, fees, and interchange. Finance charges are the periodic interest costs associated with an unpaid balance at the end of a grace period. Fees include annual membership fees, late payment fees, cash advance transaction fees, and over-limit fees. Interchange is the fee paid by merchants and passed to the card-issuing bank for completing the transaction.

- *Loss rates* are evaluated relative to the seasoning of the pool and the marketing and underwriting strategies of the originator. Rating agencies pay particular attention to estimated and actual loss rates when settling on credit enhancement levels and monitoring securities for potential ratings actions.

- The *monthly payment rate* includes monthly collections of principal, finance charges, and fees paid by the borrower. Payment rate monitoring is focused on principal collections since it is principal repayments that will be used to pay down the investor's outstanding principal.

- The *purchase rate* is the amount of new charges transferred to the trust each month from the designated accounts as a percent of the receivables outstanding. New purchases keep the amount of principal receivables in the trust from falling. If the pool balance falls below a minimum, the seller is usually required to assign additional accounts to the pool.

Other items of interest are finance charge and principal allocations among the various interests in the trust and, for floating rate issues, coupon rates. Should any of the aforementioned indicators show prolonged signs of deterioration by tripping a preset trigger, early amortization would begin.

Common early amortization triggers include:

- A reduction in the portfolio yield (net of defaults) below a base rate (investor coupon plus the servicing fee) averaged over a three-month period.
- A reduction in the seller's interest below a fixed percentage of the total principal receivables outstanding.

- A failure of the seller, servicer, or the credit enhancement provider to perform as required by the terms of the pooling and servicing agreement.

An early return of principal is not always welcomed by investors, so a well-structured agreement should balance the need for predictable repayment with the need to maintain satisfactory credit quality.

## Impact of Securitization on Bank Issuers

Properly managed, securitization enables a bank to originate a higher volume of assets while managing deposit insurance and reserve requirement costs; reducing credit risk, liquidity risk, and interest rate risk; diversifying funding sources and tenors; and maintaining (and expanding) customer relationships. The net effects of these benefits can be improved return-on-asset and return-on-equity ratios, enhanced customer service, and reduced exposure to concentration risks.

Examiners should be aware, however, that management at some banks may overestimate the risk transfer of securitization or may underestimate the commitment and resources required to effectively manage the process. Such mistakes may lead to highly visible problems during the life of the transaction that could impair future access to the securitization markets as a funding source. The risks faced by a bank will largely be a function of the roles they play in the transaction and the quality of the underlying assets they originate and/or service. The objective of the risk management evaluation performed by examiners should be to assess the impact of all aspects of securitization on the overall financial condition and performance of the institution.

## Process Management

Banks that have been able to exploit the full range of benefits offered by securitization typically view the process as a broad-based strategic initiative. As part of this approach they have integrated their risk management systems into all facets of the securitization process.

### New Product Evaluation

First-time securitizers should ensure that the proposed process has been thoroughly reviewed before the first transaction. The business plan for securitization (or for introducing any new product) should detail the business rationale, how existing policies should be modified, a performance measurement process, a list of potential counterparties (credit enhancers, underwriters, trustees, etc.), and assurances that the bank has adequate controls and procedures, systems, and risk analysis techniques. The business proposal should at least provide a description of:

- The proposed products, markets, and business strategy;
- The risk management implications;
- The methods to measure, monitor, and control risk;
- The accounting, tax, and regulatory implications;
- Any legal implications; and
- Any necessary system enhancements or modifications.

All relevant departments should review and approve the proposal. Key parties normally include the risk oversight function, operations, information technology, finance/accounting, legal, audit, and senior line management. A rigorous approval process for new products or activities lessens the risk that bank management may underestimate the level of due diligence required for risk management or the ongoing resources required for process management.

## Responsibility and Accountability

While ad hoc committees often form the initial steering group for a securitization transaction, proficient issuers usually assign responsibility for managing securitization to a dedicated individual or department. This manager (or group) should have the experience and skills to understand the various components of securitization and the authority to communicate and act across product and department lines. The manager should consider the effects that proposed changes in policies or procedures on origination or servicing may have on outstanding or future securitization issues. He or she should communicate observations and conclusions to senior management.

## Oversight

All risk management programs should be independently monitored and evaluated, usually by an internal audit unit or another risk control unit. The control group determines whether internal control practices are in accordance with risk management policies, whether controls are adequate, whether risk levels are accurately estimated, and whether such levels are appropriate.

To facilitate the development of internal controls, risk managers should be informed about the securitization process at the earliest possible stage. During the initial due diligence for a securitization transaction, the underwriter (often an investment banker), the rating agencies, and the independent outside accountants thoroughly review the bank's securitization process. Their review, however, takes place primarily in the early stages of the process; they do little direct review after the initial transaction is complete. At that point, the bank's internal oversight takes on vast importance.

The bank's risk control unit should report directly to a senior executive to ensure the integrity of the process. The unit, which should evaluate every role the bank has in securitization, should pay special attention to the origination and servicing operations. In the origination area, the unit should take significant samples of credit decisions, verify information sources, and track the approval process. In the servicing area, the unit should track payment processing, collections, and reporting from the credit approval decision through the management and third-party reporting process. The purpose of these reviews is to ensure that activities are consistent with policy and trust agreements and to detect operational weaknesses that leave the bank open to fraud or other problems. Risk managers often suggest policies or procedures to prevent problems, such as documenting exceptions to bank policies. Any irregularities discovered in the audits should be followed up and discussed with senior management.

## Monitoring of Securitization Transactions

Management reports should monitor the performance of the underlying asset pools for all outstanding deals. Although the bank may have sold the ownership rights and control of the assets, the bank's reputation as an underwriter or servicer remains exposed. To control the impact of deterioration in pools originated or serviced by the bank, a systematic reporting process allows management to track pool quality and performance throughout the life of the transactions.

Reports on revolving transactions (credit cards, home equity lines, etc.) should monitor:

- The portfolio's gross yield;
- Delinquencies;
- The charge-off rate;
- The base rate (investor coupon plus servicing fees);
- Monthly excess spread;
- The rolling three-month average excess spread; and
- The monthly payment rate.

Reports on securities backed by installment loans (automobiles, equipment leases, etc.) should monitor:

- The charge-off rate;
- The net portfolio yield (portfolio yield minus charge-offs);
- Delinquencies (aged);
- Principal prepayment speeds; and
- Outstanding principal compared to original security size.

### Communication with Outside Parties

To maintain market confidence, reputation, and the liquidity of securities, issuers and servicers should be able to supply accurate and timely information about the performance of underlying assets to investors, rating agencies, and investment bankers. The bank's cost of accessing the capital markets can depend on this ability. The securitization manager or management unit should regularly verify information on performance.

## Risks and Controls

Although it is common for securitization transactions to receive substantial attention early in their lives, the level of scrutiny generally declines over time. Many of the problems that institutions have experienced, such as rising delinquencies and charge-offs, inaccurate investor reporting, and bad publicity, have occurred in the later stages of the transaction. The bank should supervise and monitor a transaction for the duration of the institution's involvement.

Examiners assess banking risk relative to its impact on earnings and capital. From a supervisory perspective, risk is the potential that events, expected or unanticipated, will have an adverse impact on the bank's earnings or capital. The primary risks associated with securitization activities are reputation, strategic, credit, transaction, liquidity, and compliance. The types and levels of risk to which a particular banking organization is exposed will depend upon the organization's role or roles in the securitized transactions. The definitions of these risks and their pertinence to securitization are discussed below. For more complete definitions, see the "Bank Supervision Process" booklet of the *Comptroller's Handbook*.

## Reputation Risk

Reputation risk is the risk to earnings or capital arising from negative public opinion. This affects the institution's ability to establish new relationships or services or continue servicing existing relationships. This risk can expose the institution to litigation, financial loss, or damage to its reputation. Reputation risk is present throughout the organization and includes the responsibility to exercise an abundance of caution in dealing with its customers and community.

### Nature of Reputation Risk

Exposure to reputation risk is essentially a function of how well the internal risk management process is working in each of the other risk categories and the manner and efficiency with which management responds to external influences on bank-related transactions. Reputation risk has a "qualitative" nature, reflecting the strength of an organization's franchise value and how it is perceived by other market participants. This perception is usually tied to performance over time. Although each role a bank plays in securitization places its reputation on the line, it stakes its reputation most heavily on the quality of the underlying receivables and the efficiency of its servicing or other fiduciary operations.

Asset performance that falls short of expectations will reflect poorly on the underwriting and risk assessment capabilities of the originator. Because the asset performance of securitized pools is publicly disclosed and monitored by market participants, securitization can highlight problems that were less obvious when reported as a smaller component of overall portfolio performance.

The best evidence of positive or negative perception is how the market accepts and prices newly issued asset-backed securities. Poorly performing assets or servicing errors on existing transactions can increase the costs and decrease the profitability of future deals. Reputation as an underwriter or servicer is particularly important to issuers that intend to securitize regularly. For some issuers, negative publicity from securitization transactions may cause the market to avoid other liability as well as equity issuances.

### Managing Reputation Risk

The most effective method of controlling reputation risk is a sound business plan and a comprehensive, effective risk management and control framework that covers all aspects of securitization activities. Up-front effort will minimize the potential for unexpected errors and surprises, most of which are quite visible to public market participants.

Management of reputation risk often involves business decisions that extend beyond the technical, legal, or contractual responsibilities of the bank. For securitization activities, problems are most often associated with revolving assets. Although the bank has transferred legal liability for performance of such receivables, it is nevertheless closely associated with the assets through servicing, through replacement receivables sales, or simply by name. Decisions to protect franchise value by providing additional financial support should be made with full recognition of the potential long-term market, accounting, legal, and regulatory impacts and costs.

## Strategic Risk

Strategic risk is the risk to earnings and capital arising from adverse business decisions or improper implementation of those decisions. This risk is a function of the compatibility of an organization's strategic goals, the business strategies developed to achieve those goals, the resources deployed against those goals, and the quality of implementation. The resources needed to carry out business strategies are both tangible and intangible. They include communication channels, operating systems, delivery networks, and managerial capacities and capabilities.

## Nature of Strategic Risk

To assess a bank's strategic risk exposure, one must recognize the long-term impacts of securitization on operations, profitability, and asset/liability management. Such exposure increases if transactions are undertaken without considering the long-term internal resource requirements. For example, while the existing systems in the credit and collections department may be adequate for normal operations, securitization transactions are often accompanied by rapid growth in the volume of transactions and more timely and precise reporting requirements. At a minimum this may require improved computer systems and software and dedicated operational and treasury personnel. Business and strategic plans should delineate the long-term resources needed to handle the projected volume of securitization.

Decisions on credit quality and origination also expose a bank to strategic risk. The availability of funding, the opportunity to leverage systems and technology, and the ability to substantially increase fee income through securitization should not lure issuers into a business line about which they don't have sufficient knowledge. For example, banks that are successful at underwriting and servicing 'A' quality paper may not be as successful with 'B/C' paper, because different skills are needed to service higher risk loans. Banks that have been successful in entering new product lines are those that have first acquired the necessary expertise.

Competition is a prime source of strategic risk. Securitization provides economical funding to a far greater pool of credit originators than banks have traditionally had to compete against. The long-term effects of this greater competition may be to erode profit margins and force banks to seek further efficiencies and economies of scale. Tighter profitability margins diminish the room for error, increasing the importance of strategy. Many market participants (including banks) will be forced to find where their competitive advantages lie and what new or additional skills they need to compete.

**Managing Strategic Risk**

Before initiating a securitization transaction, management should compare the strategic and financial objectives of proposed securitization activities with the risk exposures and resource requirements. A thorough analysis would include the costs of the initial transaction and any systems or technology upgrades necessary to fulfill servicing obligations. Because securitization affects several different areas in a bank, the assessment should describe the responsibilities of each key person or department. Each manager responsible for an area involved in the securitization process should review the assessment.

# Credit Risk

Credit risk is the risk to earnings or capital arising from an obligor's failure to meet the terms of any contract with the bank or otherwise to perform as agreed. Credit risk is found in all activities where success depends upon counterparty, issuer, or borrower performance. It arises any time bank funds are extended, committed, invested, or otherwise exposed through actual or implied contractual agreements, whether on or off the balance sheet.

One of the primary benefits of securitization is its usefulness in managing credit risk exposure. For example, overall portfolio quality may improve because of the opportunity to diversify exposure to a particular industry (e.g., oil and gas, real estate, retail credit, etc.) or geographic area. Securitization structures reduce the credit exposure of the assets sold by transferring the unexpected portion of the default risk to credit enhancement providers and investors. Effective risk management requires recognizing the extent and limits of this risk transfer and planning for the capital and other resource requirements necessary to support the remaining risk levels.

**Nature of Credit Risk**

Although financial reporting and regulatory risk-based capital practices are useful indicators of the credit impact of securitization on a bank, these guidelines do not fully capture the economic dimensions of the originator's exposure to credit risk from a sale of securitized assets. Although important, an examiner's inquiry should extend beyond whether the sale of assets is accounted for on or off the balance sheet. It should assess the fundamental residual credit risks left with the bank after the transaction. In addition, the assessment should be made in the context of a total return standard rather than focusing solely on absolute loss and delinquency levels. For example, some pools, such as sub-prime automobile loans, are expected to have relatively high loss and delinquency rates. These pools, if properly underwritten, can be economically successful as long as the pricing and structure of the loans reflects the inherent risks.

A bank that sells assets in a securitization transaction confronts three main forms of credit risk:

- Residual exposure to default.
- Credit quality of the remaining on-balance-sheet portfolio.
- Possibility that it will have to provide moral recourse.

*Default Exposure.* Securitizing banks must evaluate how much default risk remains with them after a sale. Quantifying the residual default risk or contingent liability requires an in-depth review of the cash flow structure of the transaction and its third-party support. In most structures, credit risk is allocated so that the originator bears default losses up to a certain point, typically based on historic losses and projected performance. The first loss exposure assumed by the originator is a function of its acceptance of excess portfolio yield as a residual interest, that is, after the coupon and servicing expense are paid and loan losses are calculated. As pool performance deteriorates and charge-offs increase, excess spread (which could eventually return to the bank) declines.

Subject to certain structural provisions, excess spread may be diverted to fund or supplement cash collateral accounts for the benefit of investors and credit enhancers. Once excess spread is exhausted, the risks of credit default customarily shift to credit enhancers up to some additional multiple of projected losses. Only defaults above these multiples are borne by investors. As previously discussed, other protective measures, such as early amortization provisions, insulate investors and, to some extent, credit enhancers. Since losses of the magnitude required to trigger early amortization are infrequent, originators effectively absorb a substantial portion of realized losses in most securitized pools.

*Remaining Asset Quality.* Securitization readily lends itself to high-quality assets that provide a predictable, steady cash flow stream. Higher and more predictable net cash flows translate into lower credit enhancement fees and higher excess spread income. This may tempt banks to securitize the better-quality assets while keeping lower quality assets on the balance sheet. Because a bank new to the securitization markets does not have a track record with investors, it may be especially inclined to do so. If this approach becomes a habit, the bank will be required to hold more capital and loan loss reserves for the assets that remain on the books. Such an approach can compromise the integrity of loan loss reserve analyses that are based on historical performance.

*Moral Recourse.* Most prospectuses on asset-backed securities issued by banks clearly state that *the offering is not an obligation of the originating bank.* Despite this lack of legal obligation, in certain circumstances an originator may feel compelled to protect its name in the marketplace by providing support to poorly performing asset pools. Because there is some precedent in the market for preventing ratings downgrades or early amortization, many investors expect sponsors to aid distressed transactions.

Deciding to provide financial support for sold assets is difficult for banks. In addition to the immediate costs associated with steps to improve the yield on the asset pool, there may be other accounting, legal, and regulatory costs. For example, actions taken to support previously sold assets may compromise both the transaction's legal standing as a sale and the ability to treat the assets as off-balance-sheet items for GAAP and regulatory capital purposes. If this occurs, performance ratios, regulatory capital charges, and perhaps the tax treatment of the transaction may be affected.

Prudent business practice dictates that management consider all of the potential costs of providing additional enhancement to poorly performing asset pools. Not only would the bank supply direct financial support but it may also be obliged by its assumption of greater risk to meet a higher capital requirement. From a practical viewpoint, examiners should recognize that banks may decide to support outstanding securitization transactions to retain access to the funding source, even though doing so may require them to hold additional capital. For example, if bankers were to allow early amortization, they might need to obtain both new funding for the assets returning to the balance sheet and additional risk-based capital. Although such a decision is for management to make, examiners should ensure appropriate risk-based capital levels are maintained for the risks assumed. (See the risk-based capital discussion under "Other Issues" for additional guidance.)

*Other Credit Quality Issues.* Banks can also assume credit risk exposure from securitized asset pools by becoming a credit enhancer for assets originated by a third party. Doing so exposes a bank to credit risk from a pool of loans it had no part in originating. So credit-enhancing banks must understand the transaction structure and perform adequate due diligence, especially when exceptions to underwriting policies and overrides are involved.

## Managing Credit Risk

Because originating banks absorb most of the expected losses from both on-balance-sheet and securitized pools, sound underwriting standards and practices remain the best overall protection against excessive credit exposure. These banks should include experienced credit personnel in the strategic and operating decision-making process. Investment-banker, marketing, or other volume-oriented parties should not drive the process. Often, sustained periods of dramatic growth, aggressive teaser rates, and liberal balance transfer strategies are indications of an easing of underwriting standards. No matter how competitive the market, decisions on credit quality should be careful ones. In effective risk management systems, audit or credit review functions regularly test the lenders' compliance with underwriting standards for both on- and off-balance-sheet credits.

Most banks recognize the broad effects of securitization on credit risk and strategically attempt to ensure that sold and retained loans are of the same general quality. To protect against the tendency to loosen underwriting standards for pools that lenders believe may be sold, many banks require that all loans be subject to the same loan policy and approval process. To minimize the potential that the quality of securitized and retained loans differ, many banks employ a random selection process to ensure that every pool of assets reflects the overall quality of the portfolio and underwriting standards. If a business decision is made to choose a specific quality of loans for sale, special precautions are warranted.

If the sold loans are of *higher* quality than retained loans, then management should acknowledge the increased level of on-balance-sheet risk by ensuring that the bank's capital level and allowance for loan and lease losses are maintained at appropriate levels. If sold loans are to be *lower* quality than retained loans, the business and/or capital plans should acknowledge the increased vulnerability to moral recourse.

## Other Credit Issues

*Automated Underwriting Systems.* Because securitization rewards economies of scale and allows a bank to originate a greater volume of receivables, many originators now use automated underwriting systems such as credit scoring and the electronic services of ratings companies such as Dun & Bradstreet. The objective is to speed credit approvals by allowing computers to accept (or reject) the large number of applications that are well within (or outside) the underwriting guidelines. Marginal applications are then processed individually. Use of these systems also improves the ability to predict and model pool performance, which in turn can lower the cost of credit enhancement and security coupon rates.

In addition to loan quality problems, poorly designed automated underwriting and scoring systems can adversely affect some borrowers or groups of borrowers. The bank's CRA policy, or loan policy, should address the needs of low- to moderate-income members of the trade area. The bank should be aware of the possibility of economic redlining, which could be caused, in part, by its desire to conform to the criteria handed down by the secondary market. Compliance reviews should include originations for securitization to ensure compliance with CRA. Automated scoring systems should be managed like other risk management models. For example, they should be tested periodically for continued relevance and validity.

*Stress Testing of Securitized Pools.* Many banks use cash flow models to simulate the structure and performance of their securitized asset pools. These models trace funds through the proposed transaction structure, accounting for the source and distribution of cash flows under many possible scenarios. Because the cash flows from any pool of assets can vary significantly depending on economic and market events, banks often subject proposed structures to severe stress-testing to predict the loss exposures of investors and credit enhancers under most-likely and worst-case scenarios.

The effectiveness of models used to predict the performance of loan pools depends on disciplined adherence to clear underwriting standards for individual loans. Although a potentially powerful tool, models can be misused, become outdated, or skew results because of inaccurate or incomplete information. Any of these factors may cause projections to vary from the actual performance of the asset pool. To control potential weaknesses, management should back-test model results regularly, revalidate the logic and algorithms, and ensure the integrity of data entry/capture and assumptions.

*Vintage Analysis.* Another technique used to monitor loan quality and estimate future portfolio performance is vintage analysis. This type of analysis tracks delinquency, foreclosure, and loss ratios for similar products over comparable time periods. The objective is to identify sources of credit quality problems (such as weak or inappropriate underwriting standards) early so that corrective measures can be taken. Because loan receivables often do not reach peak delinquency levels until they have seasoned for several months, tracking the payment performance of seasoned loans over time allows the bank to evaluate the quality of newer receivables over comparable time periods and to forecast the impact that aging will have on portfolio performance.

*Disclosure vs. Confidentiality.* Most commercial loan files contain a substantial amount of nonpublic information. Much of this information is confidential. Although banks want to honor this confidence, they also feel obligated to disclose all the material information that a prospective investor should know. The problem is less daunting with homogeneous consumer loan products that lend themselves to aggregate performance analysis than it is in the growing markets for small business loans and other commercial loan products.

Bank policy on securitization of commercial loans should address the disclosure of confidential information provided by borrowers that are privately owned companies. The bank should obtain legal advice concerning what information should be disclosed or not disclosed about an issue of securitized loans. Bank counsel should also sign off on decisions whether to inform borrowers of the disclosure of nonpublic information. To avoid problems with large commercial borrowers, bank management may wish to routinely obtain an acknowledgment or release from customers.

# Transaction Risk

Transaction risk is the risk to earnings or capital arising from problems with service or product delivery. This risk is a function of internal controls, information systems, employee integrity, and operating processes. Transaction risk exists in all products and services.

For most securitized asset sales, the responsibility for servicing the assets is retained by the originator. This obligation usually extends throughout the life of the issued securities. Since the fee associated with servicing the portfolio is typically fixed, the risk of inefficiency from an operational point of view is retained by the originator. The length of the obligation and the volume-driven nature of these activities increase the possibility that banks, especially those with limited securitization experience, will overestimate their capacity to meet obligations, will underestimate the associated costs, or both.

## Nature of Transaction Risk

The pooling and servicing agreement is the primary document defining the servicers' responsibilities for most securitization transactions. Transaction risk exposure increases when servicers do not fully understand or fulfill their responsibilities under the terms of this agreement. Servicing difficulties, such as incorrect loan and payment processing, inefficient collection of delinquent payments, or inaccurate investor reporting, expose the servicer to transaction risk. Effective servicing helps to ensure that receivables' credit quality is maintained. The main obligations assumed by the servicing bank are transaction processing, performance reporting, and collections.

*Transaction Processing.* Processing problems can occur when existing bank systems, which were designed to service volumes and types of loans that met certain portfolio objectives and constraints, are now subject to larger volumes or unanticipated loan types. Excessive volume may overextend systems and contribute to human error.

For most deals, the servicer agrees to service and administer the receivables in accordance with its customary practices and guidelines. The servicer also has the responsibility and authority to make payments to and withdrawals from deposit accounts that are governed by the documents. Servicers are typically paid a fixed percentage of the invested amount for their obligation to service the receivables (often between 1.5 percent and 2.5 percent for consumer products such as credit cards). Many bank servicers are highly rated and are able, under the pooling and servicing agreement, to commingle funds until one business day before the distribution date. Those lacking short-term, unsecured ratings of 'A-1' or better must customarily deposit collections in an eligible deposit account at another institution within one or two business days of receipt.

*Reporting.* Bank management, investors, and rating agencies all require that the performance of security pools be reported accurately and in a timely manner. Such reporting can be an especially difficult challenge for first-time issuers or for banks without integrated systems. For example, reporting difficulties have occurred when lead banks or holding companies have attempted to pool loans from various affiliates with different processing and reporting systems, or when bank-sponsored conduits have pooled receivables from various third-party originators. Servicing agreements are usually specific about the timing of payment processing and the types and structures of required reports, and trustees and investors have little tolerance for errors or delays.

*Collections.* A bank may also be exposed to transaction risk when its systems or personnel are not compatible with new types of borrowers or new products. Although securitization often provides incentives to expand activity beyond traditional markets and products, the staff members of some banks have done business only with certain customer types or are used to considerable flexibility in dealing with customers, particularly in workout situations. These bankers may have difficulties adjusting to the restrictions or specific requirements of securitization agreements. For example, the decision to compete for market share by expanding into markets for borrowers with poor credit histories may require a change in collection methods. Front-line relationship managers may be uncomfortable with the labor-intensive methods necessary for long-term success in this market segment, and pool performance may suffer.

The increased transaction volumes and risk transfers associated with securitization have, in some ways, depersonalized the lending and collections process. For example, limiting bankers' ability to work out problems with customers may pose special problems. In order to maintain strong relationships with customers, some bankers may wish to ignore the limits of typical pool requirements in renegotiating repayment terms and collateral positions. If longstanding customer relationships are valuable enough, some bankers may decide to repurchase securitized loans and draw up more flexible workout terms. Management should recognize that decisions to repurchase loans may compromise "sales treatment" for some transactions.

*Liquidity Enhancement.* As part of the servicing agreement, seller/servicers are sometimes obligated to enhance the liquidity of receivables securitized. The purpose of doing so is *not* to protect against deterioration in the credit quality of the underlying receivables but rather to ensure that the security issuer (the trust) will have sufficient funds to pay obligations as scheduled. Funding becomes necessary when the due date of payments to investors arrives before sufficient collections accrue. This liquidity enhancement requires a servicer to make cash advances to the trustee on behalf of obligors who may not pay as scheduled or estimated. However, a servicer can usually exempt itself from making such advances by formally determining that the funds would not be recoverable. In many cases the accuracy of a servicer's "recovery determination" is reviewable by the trustee. If the servicer does advance funds against receivables that later default for credit quality purposes, the liquidity provider obtains the investor's rights to use proceeds from the credit enhancement to repay any advances it has made.

## Managing Transaction Risk

The effective management of servicing obligations requires a thorough understanding of the securitization process and especially the associated information and technology requirements. To reduce the bank's exposure to transaction risk, management should evaluate staffing, skill levels, and the capacity of systems to handle the projected type and volume of transactions.

The largest hurdle is typically the development of system enhancements that provide timely and accurate information on both the securitized loan pools and the bank's remaining portfolio. Reports should be designed and modified as necessary to allow servicing managers to evaluate the performance of specific loan types and to monitor continuing performance. Quality control of the servicing operation may require periodic reports and an analysis of borrowers' complaints, which are usually about servicing problems or loan quality. The servicer should also have adequate insurance against errors and omissions. The volume and types of loans serviced by the bank will dictate the amount of insurance.

To mitigate transaction risk exposure, pooling and servicing agreements usually require independent accounting reviews of the servicer at least annually. These reviews result in written opinions on the servicer's compliance with the documents and on the adequacy of its operating policies and procedures. Efficient servicers supplement this annual external review of operations with periodic internal reviews.

Servicing capabilities, which should be a subject of long-range technology planning, should keep pace with projected volumes. Plans for servicing should prepare the company to resolve possible incompatibilities of loan systems within the company, as well as incompatibilities of internal systems with pools purchased from third parties. Every bank should have a back-up system, which should be tested at least annually. At a minimum, the guidelines provided in Banking Circular 177, "Corporate Contingency Planning," must be followed.

*Liquidity Enhancement.* In view of the responsibilities and liabilities that may accrue to the servicer as a liquidity provider, a formal policy should be developed that determines how the bank will respond to situations that require funds to be advanced. Servicers who provide back-up liquidity will often protect against exposure to deteriorating asset quality by defining a borrowing base of eligible (performing) assets against which they will advance. They may require that there be no existing breach of covenants or warranties on the loans, and that neither borrowers nor seller have initiated bankruptcy proceedings. Liquidity providers will often have senior liens on the eligible assets, or will otherwise be senior to credit enhancement facilities or other obligations of the issuer.

# Liquidity Risk

Liquidity risk is the risk to earnings or capital arising from a bank's inability to meet its obligations when they come due, without incurring unacceptable losses. Liquidity risk includes the inability to manage unplanned decreases or changes in funding sources. Liquidity risk also arises from the bank's failure to recognize or address changes in market conditions that affect the ability to liquidate assets quickly and with minimal loss in value.

Given adequate planning and an efficient process structure, securitization can provide liquidity for balance sheet assets, as well as funding for leveraging origination capacity. This not only provides banks with a ready source of managed liquidity, but it increases their access to, and presence in, the capital markets.

## Nature of Liquidity Risk

The securitization of assets has significantly broadened the base of funds providers available to banks and created a more liquid balance sheet. Too much reliance on a single funding vehicle, however, increases liquidity risk.

Banks must prepare for the possible return of revolving-credit receivable balances to the balance sheet as a result of either scheduled or early amortization. The primary risk is the potential that large asset pools could require balance sheet funding at unexpected or inopportune times. This risk threatens banks that do not correlate maturities of individual securitized transactions with overall planned balance sheet growth. This exposure is heightened at banks that seek to minimize securitization costs by structuring each transaction at the maturity offering the lowest cost, without regard to maturity concentrations or potential long-term funding requirements.

A second concern is unmitigated dependence on securitization markets to absorb new asset-backed security issues — a mistake that banks originating assets specifically for securitization are more likely to make. Such a bank may allocate only enough capital to support a "flow" of assets to the securitization market. This strategy could cause funding difficulties if circumstances in the markets or at the bank were to force the institution to hold assets on its books.

---

## Managing Liquidity Risk

The implications of securitization for liquidity should be factored into a bank's day-to-day liquidity management and its contingency planning for liquidity. Each contemplated asset sale should be analyzed for its impact on liquidity both as an individual transaction and as it affects the aggregate funds position.

Liquidity management issues include:

- The volume of securities scheduled to amortize during any particular period;
- The plans for meeting future funding requirements (including when such requirements are expected);
- The existence of early amortization triggers;
- An analysis of alternatives for obtaining substantial amounts of liquidity quickly; and
- Operational concerns associated with reissuing securities.

The bank should monitor all outstanding transactions as part of day-to-day liquidity management. The bank should develop systems to ensure that management is forewarned of impending early amortization triggers, which are often set off by three successive months of negative cash flow (excess spread) on the receivables pool. Management should be alerted well in advance of an approaching trigger so that preventive actions can be considered. Thus forewarned, management should also factor the maturity and potential funding needs of the receivables into shorter-term liquidity planning.

Contingency planning should anticipate potential problems and be thorough enough to assume that, during a security's amortization phase, management will be required to find replacement funding for the full amount of the receivables. Plans should outline various funding alternatives, recognizing that a complete withdrawal from the securitization market or a cutback in lending could affect the bank's reputation with investors and borrowers.

# Compliance Risk

Compliance risk is the risk to earnings or capital arising from violations or nonconformance with laws, rules, regulations, prescribed practices, or ethical standards. Compliance risk also arises in situations where the laws or rules governing certain bank products or activities of the bank's clients may be ambiguous or untested. Compliance risk also exposes the institution to fines, civil money penalties, payment of damages, and the voiding of contracts. Compliance risk can lead to a diminished reputation, reduced franchise value, limited business opportunities, lessened expansion potential, and lack of contract enforceability.

Consumer laws and regulations, including fair lending and other anti-discrimination laws, affect the underwriting and servicing practices of banks even if they originate loans with the intent to securitize them. Management should ensure that staff involved in the underwriting and servicing functions (including collections) comply fully with these laws and regulations. Examiner's should refer to the *Comptroller's Handbook for Compliance* for detailed guidance on identifying and assessing compliance risk in the lending process.

# Other Issues

There are two significant events, effective January 1, 1997, that affect the capital and financial reporting requirements for sales of assets associated with securitization transactions. First, the Federal Financial Institutions Examination Council (FFIEC) decided that banks should follow generally accepted accounting principles (GAAP) for their quarterly reports of condition and income (call reports). Second, The Financial Accounting Standards Board (FASB) adopted Financial Accounting Standard 125, "Accounting for Transfers and Servicing of Financial Assets and Extinguishments of Liabilities" (FAS 125). Both of these changes affect how banks must recognize revenue and maintain capital for securitization transactions.

### Accounting

Under GAAP, the applicable accounting guidance for asset transfers in a securitization transaction is FAS 125. Although primarily concerned with

---

differentiating sales from financing treatment, FAS 125 also describes how to properly account for servicing assets and other liabilities in securitization transactions. FAS 125 applies to all types of securitized assets, including auto loans, mortgages, credit card loans, and small business loans. FAS 125 replaced previous accounting guidance including FAS 77, "Reporting by Transferor for Transfers of Receivables with Recourse," FAS 122, "Accounting for Mortgage Servicing Rights," and various guidance issued by FASB's Emerging Issues Task Force.

Generally, the accounting treatment for an asset transfer under FAS 125 is determined by whether legal control over the financial assets changes. Specifically, a securitization transaction will qualify for "sales" treatment (i.e., removal from the seller's reported financial statements) if the transaction meets the following conditions:

- The transferred assets are isolated from the seller (that is, they are beyond the reach of the seller and its creditors, even in bankruptcy or other receivership);

- The buyer can pledge or exchange the transferred assets, or the buyer is a qualifying special-purpose entity and the holders of the beneficial interests in that entity have the right to pledge or exchange those interests; and

- The seller does not retain effective control over the transferred assets through an agreement that

    - Both entitles and obligates it to repurchase the assets before maturity, or
    - Entitles it to repurchase transferred assets that are not readily obtainable in the market.

If the securitization transaction meets the FAS 125 criteria, the seller:

- Removes all transferred assets from the balance sheet;
- Recognizes all assets obtained and liabilities incurred in the transaction at fair value; and
- Recognizes in earnings any gain or loss on the sale.

Any recourse obligation in a transaction qualifying for sales treatment should be recorded as a liability, at fair value, and subtracted from the cash received to determine the gain or loss on the transaction. If the "sales treatment" criteria are not met, the transferred assets remain on the balance sheet and the transaction is accounted for as a secured borrowing (and no gain or loss is recognized).

*A Sample Transaction.* The adoption of GAAP for regulatory reporting purposes and FAS 125 change the accounting for asset sales associated with securitization transactions. Certain gains or losses that were deferred under previous regulatory accounting practices are now recognized on the sale date.

The following is an *example* of the accounting entries a seller might make when transferring credit card receivables to a master trust:

**The initial sales transaction:**

| | |
|---|---|
| Principal amount of initial receivables pool: | $120,000 |
| Carrying amount net of specifically allocated loss reserve | $117,000 |
| Servicing fee (based on outstanding receivables balance) | 2% |
| Up-front transaction costs: | $ 600 |
| Seller's interest: | $ 20,000 |
| Value of servicing asset | $ 1,500 |

**Transaction structure**

| | Fair Value* | Allocated % of total Fair Value | Carrying Amount | Portion Sold | Portion Retained |
|---|---|---|---|---|---|
| Class A | $ 100,000 | (117/124.5) | $ 93,976 | $ 93,976 | |
| Seller's Interest | $ 20,000 | (117/124.5) | $ 18,795 | | $ 18,795 |
| IO Strip** | $ 3,000 | (117/124.5) | $ 2,819 | | $ 2,819 |
| Servicing | $ 1,500 | (117/124.5) | $ 1,410 | | $ 1,410 |
| Total | $124,500 | | $117,000 | $ 93,796 | $ 23,024 |

*Must be estimated. See guidance under "Estimating Fair Value."

**An IO (interest-only) strip is a contractual right to receive some or all of the interest due on an interest bearing financial instrument. In a securitization transaction, it refers to the present value of the expected future excess spread from the underlying asset pool.

The journal entries to record the initial transaction on the books of the bank are:

|  |  | Debits |  |
|---|---|---|---|
| Entry #1. | Cash | $99,400 | ($100,000 - 600) |
|  | IO Strip | 2,819 |  |
|  | Servicing Asset | 1,410 |  |
|  | Seller's Certificate | 18,795 |  |

|  | Credits |
|---|---|
| Net Carrying Amount of Loans | $117,000 |
| Pretax Gain | 5,424 |

(To record securitization transaction by recognizing assets retained and by removing assets sold.)

FAS 125 requires the seller to record the IO strip at its allocated cost. However, since the IO strip is treated like a marketable equity security, it must be carried at fair market value throughout its life. Therefore, adjusting entries are necessary if the asset's estimated value changes. The following journal entry represents the recognition of an increase in the fair value of the asset. (The reverse of this entry would occur if the periodic estimate found that the value had declined or been impaired.)

| Entry #2. | IO Strip | $181 |  |
|---|---|---|---|
|  | Equity |  | $181 |

(To measure an IO strip categorized as an available-for-sale security at its fair market value as required under FAS 115).

As the bank receives cash associated with excess spread from the trust, the effect of the journal entries is to increase cash and reduce the amount of the IO strip. In effect, the entry would be:

| Entry #3. | Cash | $10 |  |
|---|---|---|---|
|  | IO Strip |  | $10 |

(To recognize cash "excess spread" from the trust.)

If the transaction meets the FAS 125 sales criteria, a selling bank should recognize the servicing obligation (asset or liability) and any residual interests in the securitized loans retained (such as the IO strip and the seller's certificate). The bank should also recognize as assets or liabilities any written or purchased options (such as recourse obligations), forward commitments, or other derivatives (e.g., commitments to deliver additional receivables during the revolving period of a securitization), or any other rights or obligations resulting from the transaction.

*Estimating Fair Value.* FAS 125 guidance states that the fair value of an asset (or liability) is the amount for which it could be bought or sold in a current transaction between willing parties — that is, in other than a forced liquidation sale. Quoted market prices in active markets are the best evidence of fair value and, if available, shall be used as the basis for the pricing.

Unfortunately, it is unlikely that a securitizer will find quoted market prices for most of the financial assets and liabilities that arise in a securitization transaction. Accordingly, estimation is necessary. FAS 125 says that if quoted market prices are not available, the estimate of fair value shall be based on the best information available. Such information includes prices for similar assets and liabilities and the results of valuation techniques such as:

- The present value of estimated expected future cash flows using a discount rate commensurate with the risks involved;
- Option-pricing models;
- Matrix pricing;
- Option-adjusted spread models; and
- Fundamental analysis.

These techniques should include the assumptions about interest rates, default rates, prepayment rates, and volatility that other market participants employ in estimating value. Estimates of expected future cash flows should be based on reasonable and supportable assumptions and projections. All available evidence should be considered in developing estimates of expected future cash flows. The weight given to the evidence should be commensurate with the extent to which the evidence can be verified objectively. If a range is estimated for either the amount or timing of future cash flows, the likelihood of possible outcomes should be considered to determine the best estimate.

*Recognition of Servicing.* A servicing asset should be recorded if the contractual servicing fee more than adequately compensates the servicer. (Adequate compensation is the amount of income that would fairly compensate a substitute servicer, and includes the profit that would be required in the market place.) The value of servicing assets includes the contractually specified servicing fees, late charges, and other related fees and income, including float.

A servicing liability should be recorded when the estimated future revenues from stated servicing fees, late charges, and other ancillary revenues are not expected to adequately compensate the servicer for performing the servicing.

The recorded value of servicing rights is initially based on the fair value of the servicing asset relative to the total fair value of the transferred assets. Servicing assets must be amortized in proportion to estimated net servicing income and over the period that such income is received. In addition, servicing assets must be periodically evaluated and measured for impairment. Any impairment losses should be recognized in current period income.

According to FAS 125, servicing assets should be subsequently measured and evaluated for impairment as follows:

1.  Stratify servicing assets based on one or more of their predominant risk characteristics. The risk characteristics may include financial asset type, size, interest rate, date of origination, term, and geographic location.

2.  Recognize impairment through a valuation allowance for each individual stratum. Impairment should be recognized as the amount by which the carrying amount of a category of servicing assets exceeds its fair value. The fair value of servicing assets that have not been recognized should not be used in this evaluation.

3.  Periodically adjust the valuation allowance to reflect changes in impairment. However, appreciation in the fair value of a stratum of servicing assets over its carrying amount should not be recognized.

*Treatment of Excess Cash Flows.* The right to future income in excess of contractually stated servicing fees should be accounted for separately from the servicing asset. The right to these cash flows is treated as an interest-only strip and accounted for under FAS 115 as either an available-for-sale or trading security.

If IO strips or other receivables or retained interests in securitizations can be contractually prepaid or settled in a way that the holder might not substantially recover its recorded investment, FAS 125 requires that they be measured at fair value and that the treatment be similar to that given available-for-sale and trading securities under FAS 115. Accordingly, these items are initially recorded at allocated fair value. (Allocating fair value refers to apportioning the previous carrying amount of the transferred assets between the assets sold and the interests retained by the seller based on their relative fair values at the date of transfer. See example entry #1.) These items are periodically adjusted to their estimated fair value (example entry #2) based on their expected cash flows.

*Recognition of Fees.* The accounting treatment of fees associated with loans that will be securitized should be in accordance with FAS 91, "Accounting for Nonrefundable Fees and Costs Associated with Originating or Acquiring Loans and Initial Direct Costs of Leases" and FAS 65, "Accounting for Certain Mortgage Banking Enterprises." In accordance with these statements' standards for pools of loans that are held for sale, the loan origination fees and direct loan origination costs should be deferred and recognized in income when the loans are sold.

# Risk-Based Capital[4]

## Asset Sales without Recourse

Securitization can have important implications for a bank's risk-based capital requirement. (For a more complete discussion of OCC risk-based capital requirements, see the "Capital and Dividends" section of the *Comptroller's Handbook*.) If asset sales meet the "sale" requirements of FAS 125 and the assets are sold without recourse, the risk-based capital standards do not require the seller to maintain capital for the assets securitized. The primary attraction of securitization for bank issuers (notwithstanding the wealth of liquidity inherent in selling loans quickly and efficiently for cash) is the ability to avoid capital requirements while realizing considerable financial benefits (e.g., servicing fees, excess servicing income, and origination fees). Several of the "pure play" or monoline banks have off-balance-sheet, securitized assets that are several times larger than their on-balance-sheet loan amounts.

Although the risk-based capital standards are heavily weighted toward credit risk, a bank's capital base must also be available to absorb losses from other types of risk, such as funding source concentrations, operations, and liquidity risk. For this reason, it is prudent for banks to evaluate all of the exposures associated with securitizing assets, especially revolving assets such as credit cards and home equity lines of credit for which the bank retains a close association with the borrower even after a specific receivable balance has been sold.

Using models or other methods of analysis, a bank should allocate the appropriate amount of capital to support these risks. At least two major off-balance-sheet risk areas pertinent to securitization are not specifically discussed in the minimum capital requirements of risk-based capital:

- Servicing obligations.
- Liquidity risk associated with revolving asset pools.

---

4    At the time of this writing there are a number of pending regulations that affect capital (servicing assets, recourse, small business recourse, etc.). The reader should refer to 12 CFR 3 and "Instructions for the Consolidated Reports of Condition and Income" for definitive capital regulations and guidance.

*Servicing Obligations.* Securitization is a volume business that rewards economies of scale. The amount of capital support should be commensurate with the expected transaction volumes, the nature of the transactions (revolving or amortizing), the technology requirements, and the complexity of the collections process. A bank should consider increasing capital for servicing if bank personnel are not experienced with the asset and borrower types anticipated, the bank is offering a new product or entering a new business line, or the complexity of the servicing is growing.

*Liquidity Risks.* Securitization transactions involving revolving assets (for example, credit cards and home equity lines of credit) pose more liquidity risk than amortizing assets such as automobile loans. When a revolving-asset securitization matures, the bank must either roll any new receivables into another securitization or find another way to fund the assets. While most banks will not find it difficult to access the securitization markets in normal times, the risk of overall market disruption does exist. In addition, if a bank's financial condition or capacity to provide servicing deteriorates, access to the markets may be limited or using them may not be cost effective. These possibilities should be reflected in determining capital adequacy.

*Other Factors.* Other factors not related to credit may expose a bank to additional risk, such as representations and warranties provided by the seller, and some kinds of obligations associated with acting as a trustee or advisor for a transaction. These may vary with specific transactions and should be included in any analysis of capital adequacy.

*Capital Reserves.* When an issuer securitizes receivables, it usually reverses the bad debt reserves previously held against the receivables and takes that amount into income. Often, at the time of sale, issuers will use these freed-up reserves to set up new capital reserves for potential exposures associated with securitization transactions. While these new reserves are a healthy recognition that all risk exposures are not eliminated when assets are securitized, the capital allocation for exposures to off-balance-sheet securitization transactions should specifically reflect the nature and volume of the remaining exposures. These transaction, liquidity, and other risks may not be identical to the credit risk that has been transferred, and the capital analysis and resulting reserve decisions should focus on actual risk exposure.

## Asset Sales with Recourse

Generally, the risk-based capital requirements for assets transferred with recourse were not changed by the adoption of GAAP for regulatory reporting purposes on January 1, 1997. Guidance for the accounting and risk-based capital treatment of asset sales with recourse can be found in 12 CFR 3, appendix A, section 3(b)(1)(B)(iii), with accompanying footnote; in the instructions for the preparation of the consolidated reports of condition and income (the call reports); and in periodic interpretive letters issued by the regulatory agencies. These guidelines address the determination of recourse in an asset sale, the associated risk-based capital requirements, and the treatment of limited, or "low-level," recourse transactions.

*Recourse Determination.* In securitization activities, "recourse" typically refers to the risk of loss that a bank retains when it sells assets to a trust or other special-purpose entity established to issue asset-backed securities. The general rule is that a transfer that qualifies for sales treatment under GAAP does not require risk-based capital support provided the transferring bank:

1. Does not retain risk of loss on the transferred assets from any source, and

2. Is not obligated to any party for the payment of principal or interest on the assets transferred resulting from:

    a. Default on principal or interest by the obligor of the underlying instrument or from any other deficiencies in the obligor's performance.

    b. Changes in the market value of the assets after they have been transferred.

    c. Any contractual relationship between the seller and purchaser incident to the transfer that, by its term, could continue after final payment, default, or other termination of the assets transferred.

    d. Any other cause.

---

If risk or obligation for payment of principal or interest is retained by, or may revert to, the seller in an asset transfer that qualifies for sale treatment under GAAP, the transaction *must* be considered an "asset sale with recourse" for risk-based capital purposes.

Two exceptions to the general recourse rule do not by themselves cause a transaction to be treated as a sale with recourse. These exceptions are contractual provisions that:

- Provide for the return of the assets to the seller in instances of incomplete documentation or fraud.

- Allow the purchaser a specific period of time to determine that the assets transferred are as represented by the seller and to return deficient paper to the seller.

Assets transferred in transactions that do not qualify as sales under GAAP should continue to be reported as assets on the call report balance sheet and are subject to regulatory capital requirements.

Most transactions that involve recourse are governed by contracts written at the time of sale. These contracts set forth the terms and conditions under which the purchaser may compel payment from the seller. In some instances of recourse a bank assumes risk of loss without an explicit contractual agreement or in amounts exceeding a specified contractual limit. A bank suggests that it may have granted *implicit* recourse by taking certain actions subsequent to the sale. Such actions include: a) providing voluntary support for a securitization by selling assets to a trust at a discount from book value; b) exchanging performing for nonperforming assets; c) infusing additional cash into a spread account or other collateral account; or d) supporting an asset sale in other ways that impair the bank's capital. Proving the existence of implicit recourse is often a complex and fact-specific process. Therefore, the OCC expects that the general test of loss retention and capital impairment, supplemented by periodic interpretations as structures and asset-types evolve, will be the most effective method of determining the existence of recourse in securitization transactions.

*Risk-Based Capital Treatment.* Asset sales with recourse are reported on the call report in Schedule RC-L, "Off-Balance-Sheet Items," and Schedule RC-R, "Regulatory Capital." Under the risk-based capital standards, assets sold with recourse are risk-weighted using two steps. First, the full outstanding amount of assets sold with recourse is converted to an on-balance-sheet credit equivalent amount using a 100 percent credit conversion factor, except for certain low-level recourse transactions (described below) and small business obligations transferred with recourse. Second, the credit equivalent amount is assigned to the appropriate risk-weight category according to the obligor or, if relevant, the guarantor or the nature of the collateral.

*Low-Level Recourse Transactions.* According to the risk-based capital standards, the amount of risk-based capital that must be maintained for assets transferred with recourse should not exceed the maximum amount of recourse for which a bank is contractually liable under the recourse agreement. This rule applies to transactions in which a bank contractually limits its risk of loss or recourse exposure to less than the full effective minimum risk-based capital requirement for the assets transferred. The low-level recourse provisions may apply to securitization transactions that use contractual cash flows (e.g., interest-only strips receivable and spread accounts), retained subordinated interests, or retained securities (e.g., collateral invested amounts and cash collateral accounts) as credit enhancements. If the low-level recourse rule applies to these credit enhancements, the maximum contractual dollar amount of the bank's recourse exposure, and therefore that amount of risk-based capital that must be maintained, is generally limited to the amount carried as an asset on the balance sheet in accordance with GAAP. The call report instructions for Schedule RC-R provide specific guidance for the reporting and capital requirements for low-level recourse transactions.

1. To determine the quantity of risk and the quality of risk management by assessing whether the bank is properly identifying, measuring, monitoring, and controlling the risks associated with its securitization activities.

2. To determine whether the bank's strategic or business plan for asset securitization adequately addresses resource needs, capital requirements, and profitability objectives.

3. To determine whether asset securitization policies, practices, procedures, objectives, internal controls, and audit functions are adequate.

4. To determine that securitization activities are properly managed within the context of the bank's overall risk management process.

5. To determine the quality of operations and the adequacy of MIS.

6. To determine compliance with applicable laws, rulings, regulations, and accounting practices.

7. To determine the level of risk exposure presented by asset securitization activities and evaluate that exposure's impact on the overall financial condition of the bank, including the impact on capital requirements and financial performance.

8. To initiate corrective action when policies, practices, procedures, objectives, or internal controls are deficient, or when violations of law, rulings, or regulations have been noted.

Many of the steps in these procedures require examiners to gather information from or review information with examiners in other areas, particularly those responsible for originating assets used in securitized pools (e.g., retail lending, mortgage banking, credit card lending). To avoid duplicating examination procedures already being performed in these areas, examiners should discuss and share examination data related to asset securitization with examiners from these other areas before beginning these procedures.

Examiners should cross-reference information obtained from other areas in their examination work papers. When information is not available from other examiners, it should be requested directly from the bank. The final decision on the scope of the examination and the most appropriate way to obtain information rests with the examiner-in-charge (EIC).

The examination procedures in the first section ("Overview") will help the examiner determine how the bank securitizes and the general level of management and board oversight. The procedures in the second section ("Functions") supplement the "Overview" section and will typically be used for more in-depth reviews of operational areas. The procedures in "Overall Conclusions" (#s 67-71) should be completed for each examination.

## Overview

1.    Obtain and review the following documents:

      ☐    Previous examination findings related to asset securitization and management's response to those findings.
      ☐    Most recent risk assessment profile of the bank.
      ☐    Most recent internal/external audits addressing asset securitization and management's response to significant deficiencies.
      ☐    Supervisory Monitoring System (SMS) reports.
      ☐    Scope memorandum issued by the bank EIC.

☐ Strategic or business plan for asset securitization.

☐ All written policies or procedures related to asset securitization.

☐ A description of the risk measurement and monitoring system for securitization activities and a copy of all related MIS reports. (Measurement systems may include tracking reports, exposure reports, valuation reports, and profitability analyses. See the examination procedures under "Management Information Systems" for additional details.)

☐ A summary or outline of all outstanding asset-backed issuances. Document for the permanent work paper file information for each outstanding security including:

- The origination date, original deal amount, current outstanding balance, legal maturity, expected maturity, maturity type (hard bullet, soft bullet, controlled `amortization, etc.), revolving period dates, current coupon rates, gross yield, loss rate, base rate, excess spread amounts (one month and three month), monthly payment rates, and the existence of any interest rate caps.

- The amount and form of credit enhancements (over-collateralization, cash collateral accounts, spread accounts, etc.).

- Performance triggers relating to early amortization events or credit enhancement levels.

☐ Copies of pooling and servicing agreements and/or series supplements for major asset types securitized or those targeted at this exam.

☐ Information detailing the potential contractual or contingent liability from guarantees, underwriting, and servicing of securitized assets.

☐ Copies of compensation programs, including incentive plans, for personnel involved in securitization activities.

☐ Current organizational chart for the asset securitization unit of the bank.

☐ A list of board and executive or senior management committees that supervise the asset securitization function, including a list of members and meeting schedules. Also, minutes documenting meetings held since the last examination should be available for review.

2. Determine whether any material changes have occurred since the last review regarding originations and purchases, servicing, or managing securitized portfolios.

3. Based on results from the previous steps and discussions with the bank EIC and other appropriate supervisors, determine the scope and objectives of the examination.

   **Select from among the following examination procedures the steps necessary to meet examination objectives. Examiners should tailor the procedures to the specific activities and risks faced by the bank. Note: Examinations will seldom require completion of all steps.**

4. As examination procedures are performed, test for compliance with established policies and confirm the existence of appropriate internal controls. Identify any area that has inadequate supervision or poses undue risk, and discuss the need to perform additional or expanded procedures with the EIC.

## Management Oversight

5. Review the bank's securitization business plan. Determine that it has been reviewed by all significant affected parties and approved by the bank's board of directors. At a minimum, the plan should address the following:

   a. The integration of the securitization program into the bank's corporate strategic plan.

   b. The integration of the securitization program into the bank's asset/liability, contingency funding, and capital plans.

   c. The integration of the securitization program into the bank's compliance review, loan review, and audit program.

   d. The specific capacities in which the bank will engage (servicer, trustee, credit enhancer, etc.).

e.    The establishment of a risk identification process.

f.    The type(s) and volume of business to be done in total (aggregate of deals in process as well as completed deals that are still outstanding).

g.    Profitability objectives.

6.    Evaluate the quality of the business plan.  Consider whether:

a.    The plan is reasonable and achievable in light of the bank's capital position, physical facilities, data processing systems capabilities, size and expertise of staff, market conditions, competition, and current economic forecasts.

b.    The feasibility analysis considers tax, legal, and resource implications.

c.    The goals and objectives of the securitization program are compatible with the overall business plan of the bank, the holding company, or both.

7.    Determine whether the bank has and is following adequate policies and operating procedures for securitization activities.  At a minimum, policies should address:

a.    Permissible securitization activities including individual responsibilities, limits, and segregation of duties.

b.    Authority levels and responsibility designations covering:

- Transaction approvals and cancellations;
- Counterparty approvals for all outside entities the bank is doing business with (originators, servicers, packagers, trustees, credit enhancers, underwriters, and investors);
- Systemic and individual transaction monitoring;
- Pricing approvals;
- Hedging and other pre-sale decisions;

- Quality standard approvals; and
- Supervisory responsibilities over personnel.

c. Exposure limits by:

- Type of transaction;
- Individual transaction dollar size;
- Aggregate transactions outstanding (because of the moral recourse implicit in the bank's name on the securities);
- Geographic concentrations of transactions (individually and in aggregate);
- Maturities of transactions (particularly important in evergreen deals, i.e., credit cards and home equity lines); and
- Originators (for purchased assets), credit enhancers, trustees, and servicers.

d. Quality standards for all transactions in which the bank plans to participate. Standards should extend to all counterparties conducting business with the bank.

e. Minimum MIS reports to be presented to senior management and the board or appropriate committees. (During reviews of applicable meeting minutes, ascertain which reports are presented and the depth of discussions held).

8. Review the organizational structure and determine who is responsible for coordinating securitization activities.

a. Determine whether the board of directors or appropriate committee and management have a separate securitization steering committee. If so, review committee minutes for significant information.

b. Determine whether decision making is centralized or delegated.

c. Determine which individuals are responsible for major decisions and where final decisions are made.

9. Determine whether, before approving a new securitization transaction, the bank requires sign-off from the following departments:

- Appropriate credit division
- Treasury or capital markets
- Audit
- Asset and liability management
- Capital planning committee
- Legal
- Liquidity management
- Operations

10. Assess the expertise and experience of management responsible for securitization activities.

   a. Conduct interviews and review personnel files and resumes to determine whether management and other key staff members possess appropriate experience or technical training to perform their assigned functions.

   b. Review management succession plans and determine whether designated successors have the necessary background and experience.

11. Review incentive plans covering personnel involved in the securitization process. Determine whether plans are oriented toward quality execution and long-run profitability rather than high-volume, short-term asset production and sales.

   a. Ensure that such plans have been approved by the board of directors or an appropriate committee.

   b. Determine that senior management and the board of directors are aware of any substantial payments or bonuses made under these plans.

12. Evaluate the pricing system used in all aspects of securitization.

    a.    Determine that the bank has a system for quantifying costs and risks (liquidity, credit, transaction, etc.) and for making incremental adjustments to compensate for the less readily quantifiable costs and risks.

    b.    Determine whether decision makers use an effective pricing system to determine whether prospective transactions will be profitable.

## Risk Management

13. Determine whether the risk management process is effective and based on timely and accurate information. Evaluate its adequacy in managing significant risks in each area of the securitization process.

    a.    Ascertain whether management has identified all significant risks in each of the bank's planned roles.

    b.    Determine how these risks are monitored and controlled.

    c.    Evaluate how controls are integrated into overall bank systems.

    d.    Evaluate management's method of allocating capital or reserves to various business units in recognition of securitization risks.

14. Determine that the bank's obligations from securitization activities have been reviewed by appropriate legal counsel.

    a.    Ensure that legal counsel has reviewed and approved any standardized documents used in the securitization process. Counsel should also review any transactions that deviate significantly from standardized documents.

    b.    If the bank is involved in issuing prospectuses or private placement memoranda, ensure that legal counsel has reviewed them. Also, ensure that operating practices require a party independent of the securitization process to check the financial and statistical information in the prospectus for accuracy.

15. Determine that the scope of credit and compliance reviews includes loans originated for securitization or purchased for that purpose.

    a. Ascertain appropriateness of scope, frequency, independence, and competency of reviews in view of the bank's activity volume and risk exposure.

    b. Credit and compliance reviews should include:

        • Loans on the bank's books and not yet securitized;
        • Loans in process of being securitized; and
        • Completed deals that bear the bank's name or in which the bank has ongoing responsibilities (servicer, trustee, etc.).

**Portfolio Management**

16. Determine whether management's assessment of the quality of loan origination and credit risk management includes *all* managed assets (receivables in securitization programs and on-balance-sheet assets). At a minimum, the assessment should include:

    a. A review of the number and dollar volume of existing past-due loans, early payment defaults, and repurchased loans from securitized asset pools. The review should also compare the bank's performance to industry, peer group averages, or both.

    b. An analysis of the cause of delinquencies and repurchases.

    c. The impact on delinquencies and losses of altered underwriting practices, new origination sources, and new products.

    d. Determination of whether repurchases or other workout actions compromised the sales status of problem credits or related assets.

17. Determine whether the bank performs periodic stress tests of securitized asset pools. Determine whether these tests:

    a. Consider the appropriate variables affecting performance according to asset or pool type.

    b. Are conducted well in advance of approaching designated early amortization triggers.

    c. Are adequately documented.

18. If third parties provide credit or liquidity enhancements for bank-sponsored asset-backed securities, determine whether their credit rating has been downgraded recently or whether their credit quality has deteriorated. If so, determine what actions the bank has taken to mitigate the impact of these events.

19. Assess whether securitization activities have been adequately integrated into liquidity planning. Consider whether:

    a. The cash flows from scheduled maturities of revolving asset-backed securities are coordinated to minimize potential liquidity concerns.

    b. The impact of unexpected funding requirements due to early amortization events are factored into contingency funding plans for liquidity.

**Internal and External Audit**

20. Review the bank's internal audit program for securitization activities. Determine whether it includes objectives, written procedures, an audit schedule, and reporting systems that are appropriate in view of the bank's volume of activity and risk exposure.

    a. Review the education, experience, and ongoing training of the internal audit staff and evaluate its expertise in auditing securitization activities.

b. Determine whether comprehensive audits of all securitization areas are conducted in a timely manner. Ensure that the scope of internal audit includes:

- An evaluation of compliance with pooling and servicing agreement requirements; and
- Periodic verification of the accuracy of both internal and external portfolio performance reports.

c. Review management's responses to audit reports for timeliness and implementation of corrective action when appropriate.

21. If the external auditors review the major operational areas involved in securitization activities, review the most recent engagement letter, external audit report, and management letter. Determine:

a. To what extent the external auditors rely on the internal audit staff and the internal audit report.

b. Whether the external auditors rendered an opinion on the effectiveness of internal controls for the major products or services related to securitization.

c. Whether management promptly and effectively responds to the external auditor's concerns and recommendations. Assess whether management makes changes to operating and administrative procedures that are appropriate responses to report findings.

## Management Information Systems

22. Review management information systems to determine whether they provide appropriate information for monitoring securitization activities.

a. Evaluate reports produced for each capacity in which the bank is involved. At a minimum, the following should be produced:

- Tracking reports to monitor overall securitization activity. Reports should include:

- Completed transactions, transactions in process, and prospective transactions;
- Exposure reports detailing exposures by specific function (credit enhancer, servicer, trustee, etc.) and by counterparties; and
- Profitability analysis by product and functional department (originations, servicing, trustees, etc.). Profitability reports should include cost-center balance sheet and earnings statements. The balance sheets should reflect the amount of capital and reserves set aside for risks within the various functions.

- Inventory reports to monitor available transaction collateral. Reports should include summaries by:

  - Product type, including outstanding and committed receivable amounts;
  - Geographic or other types of concentrations; and
  - Sale status (for transactions in process).

- Performance reports by portfolio and specific product type. Reports should reflect performance of both assets in securitized pools and total managed assets. Reports should include:

  - Credit quality (delinquencies, losses, portfolio aging, etc.);
  - Profitability (by individual transaction and product type); and
  - Performance compared with expected performance (portfolio yields, monthly principal payment rates, purchase rates, charge-offs, etc.).

b. Determine whether MIS provides sufficient detail to permit reviews for compliance with policy limits and to make appropriate disclosures on regulatory reports and other required financial statements. Evaluate whether:

- The frequency of report generation is commensurate with volume and risk exposure; and
- Reports are distributed to, and reviewed by, appropriate management, board committees, or both.

23. Determine whether investor reporting is accurate and timely. Choose a sample of outstanding transactions and compare internal performance reports with those provided to investors. Note: Examiners can supplement this procedure by comparing internal reports with information reported by external sources (such as Bloomberg, Fitch, and Moody's). Discrepancies should be brought to management's attention immediately.

## Accounting and Risk-Based Capital

24. Determine whether the bank is classifying securitization transactions appropriately as "sales" or "financings."

   a. Determine that the bank has a system to ensure that independent personnel review transactions and concur with accounting treatment.

   b. Ensure that audit has tested for proper accounting treatment as part of its normal reviews.

25. For transactions that qualify for sales treatment under FAS 125, review the written policies and procedures to determine whether they:

   a. Allocate the previous book carrying amount between the assets sold and the retained interests based on their fair market values on the date of transfer.

   b. Adjust the net proceeds received in the exchange by recording, on the balance sheet, the fair market value of any guarantees, recourse obligations, or derivatives such as put options, forward commitments, interest rate swaps, or currency swaps.

   c. Recognize gain or loss only on assets sold.

d.  Continue to carry on the balance sheet any retained interest in the transferred assets. Such balance sheet items should include servicing assets, beneficial debt or equity interests in the special-purpose entity, or retained undivided interests.

26. Determine whether the asset values and periodic impairment analyses for servicing assets and rights to future excess interest (IO strips) are consistent with FAS 125 and regulatory accounting requirements.

a.  Determine whether the bank has a reasonable method for determining fair market value of the assets.

b.  Determine whether recorded servicing and IO strip asset values are reviewed in a timely manner and adjusted for changes in market conditions.

For servicing assets, verify that:

- Servicing assets are appropriately stratified by predominant risk characteristics (e.g., asset type, interest rate, date of origination, or geographic location);
- Impairment is recognized by stratum;
- Impairment is assessed frequently (e.g., at least quarterly);
- Assumptions and calculations are documented; and
- Servicing assets are not recorded at a value greater than their original allocated cost.

For IO strip assets, verify that:

- Valuation considers changes in expected cash flows due to current and projected volatility of interest rates, default rates, and prepayment rates; and
- IO strips are recorded at fair market value consistent with available-for-sale or trading securities.

c.  Determine that servicing assets and IO strips are accorded appropriate risk-based capital treatment. Ensure that:

- Nonmortgage servicing assets are fully deducted from Tier 1 capital and risk-weighted assets. (Mortgage-related servicing assets and purchased credit card relationships may be included in Tier 1 capital; however, the total of all mortgage related servicing assets and purchased credit card relationships is limited. See 12 CFR 3 and related interpretations.)
  - Risk-based capital is allocated for the lower of the full amount of the assets transferred or the amount of the IO strip, consistent with low-level recourse rules.

27. For revolving trusts, review procedures for accounting for new sales of receivables to the trust.

   a. Verify that accrued interest on receivables sold is accounted for properly.

   b. Determine whether gain or loss is properly booked.

28. Determine whether the bank maintains capital reserves for securitized assets. Determine whether the method for calculating the reserves is reasonable. Consider:

   a. The volume and nature of servicing obligations.

   b. The potential impact on liquidity of revolving-asset pools.

   c. Other potential exposures.

**Recourse Transactions**

29. Determine whether the bank transfers loans with recourse. If so, determine whether:

   a. Written policies guide management with respect to the type and amount of recourse it can offer. Such policies should address:

      - Full or partial recourse specified in the servicing contract;

- Warranties and representations in the sale of loans, including warranties against noncompliance with consumer laws and regulations;
- Repurchase agreements in case of early default or early prepayment of securitized loans;
- Spread accounts or cash reserves;
- Vested business relationships with purchasers of whole loans or investors in asset-backed securities; and
- Environmental hazards.

    b.    Adequate management information systems exist to track all recourse obligations.

    c.    Asset sales with recourse, including low-level transactions, are reported appropriately in schedule RC-R of the report of condition and income (call report).

    d.    If recourse is limited, determine whether the bank's systems prevent it from making payments greater than its contractual obligation to purchasers.

30.    Determine whether the bank has developed written standards for refinancing, renewing, or restructuring loans previously sold in asset-backed securities transactions.  Determine whether:

    a.    The standards distinguish a borrower's valid desire to reduce an interest rate through renewal, refinancing, or restructuring designed to salvage weak credits.

    b.    The standards prevent the bank from repurchasing distressed loans from the securitized credit pool and disguising their delinquency in the bank's loan portfolio.

# Functions

The following guidelines supplement the procedures in the "Overview" section. These procedures will often be performed by product (loan) type and should be coordinated with other examination areas to avoid duplication of effort.

## Originations

31. Determine whether senior management or the board is directly involved in decisions concerning the quality and types of assets that are to be securitized as well as those to be retained on the balance sheet. Ensure that written policies:

    a.  Outline objectives relating to securitization activities.

    b.  Establish limits or guidelines for:

        - Quality of loans originated
        - Maturity of loans originated
        - Geographic dispersion of loans
        - Acceptable range of loan yields
        - Credit quality
        - Acceptable types of collateral
        - Types of loans

32. Determine whether the credit standards for loans to be securitized are the same as the ones for loans to be retained.

    a.  If not, ascertain whether management consciously made this decision and that it is clearly stated in the securitization business plan.

    b.  If higher quality loans are to be securitized in order to gain initial market acceptance, determine whether the bank limits the amount of lower quality assets it originates or retains. Also, determine whether the allowance for loan and lease losses and capital are adjusted for the higher proportion of risk in total assets.

---

c.   Determine whether there are sufficient administrative and collection personnel on hand to properly administer and collect lower quality credits.

33.   Ensure that there is a complete separation of duties between the credit approval process and loan sales/securitization effort.  Determine whether lending personnel are solely responsible for:

a.   The granting or denial of credit to customers.

b.   Credit approvals of resale counterparties.

34.   Ensure that loans to be sold or securitized are segregated or otherwise identified on the books of the originating bank.  Also, determine that the bank is following appropriate accounting standards regarding market valuation procedures on assets held for sale.

35.   If loans are granted or denied based on a credit scoring system, ascertain whether the system was developed based on empirically derived data.   Ensure that it is periodically revalidated.

36.   Determine whether the bank is making efforts to ensure that the customer base is not suffering from economic redlining.  If economic redlining is occurring, determine what actions the bank is taking to counteract these effects.  (Evidence of redlining should be immediately discussed with the EIC and/or appropriate compliance examiner.)

37.   Determine whether written policies address borrower's expectations of confidentiality and rights to financial privacy by requiring:

a.   The opinion of counsel on what matters may be disclosed.

b.   Written notice (when counsel deems it necessary) that loans may be sold in whole or pledged as collateral for asset-backed securities and that certain confidential credit information may be disclosed to other parties.

c.   When necessary, the borrower's written waiver of confidentiality.

## Purchased Loans

38. Determine whether the bank has written procedures on acquiring portfolios for possible securitization. If so, determine whether the procedures are adequate given the volume and complexity of the potential purchases.

39. Evaluate management's method of determining whether prospective asset purchases meet the quality standards represented by the seller. Ensure that the process considers whether purchased assets are compatible with the bank's data systems, administration and collection systems, credit review talent, and compliance standards, particularly consumer protection laws.

40. If the bank has recently purchased a portfolio for use in a securitization transaction, review the due diligence work papers to assess their adequacy and compliance with policy.

41. Determine whether the bank conducts postmortem reviews on acquired portfolios, and, if so, what procedures are used. Identify who receives the results and whether appropriate follow-up action is taken (changes in quality standards, due diligence procedures, etc.)

42. Ensure that operating systems segregate or otherwise identify loans being held for resale. Review accounting practices to ensure appropriate treatment of assets held for resale.

43. Evaluate the measures taken to control pipeline exposure.

    a. If pre-sales are routine, determine whether credit approval and diversification standards for purchasers are administered by people who are independent of the asset purchasing and packaging processes.

    b. Evaluate the reasonableness of limits on inventory positions that are not pre-sold or hedged.

c.  If assets held for resale are required to be hedged, ensure that controls over hedging include:

- An approved list of hedging instruments;
- Minimum acceptable correlation between the assets held for sale and the hedging vehicle;
- Maximum exposure limits to unhedged loan commitments under various interest rate simulations;
- Credit limits on forward sale exposure to a single counterparty;
- A prohibition against speculation; and
- Acceptable reporting systems for hedging transactions.

## Servicing

44.  Determine whether written policies are in place for servicing activities that:

a.  Outline objectives for the servicing department.

b.  List the types of loans that the bank is permitted to service.

c.  Specify procedures for valuing retained and purchased servicing rights.

d.  Require legal counsel to review each transaction for conflicts of interest when the bank serves in multiple capacities such as:

- Originator
- Servicer
- Trustee
- Credit enhancer
- Market maker
- Lender in other relationships to borrowers, investors, originators
- Investor

45. Determine whether MIS reports for the servicing operation provide adequate information to monitor servicing activities. Reports by asset pool or transaction should include:

   a. Activity data, including:

   - Aggregate data such as number of loans, dollar amount of loans, yield on loans.
   - Delinquency information for at least the loans that are more than 15/30/60/90 days past due;
   - Number and dollar amount of early payment default (within first three months of closing);
   - Charge-off data; and
   - Repossession costs (if applicable).

   b. Profitability information, including all costs associated with direct and indirect overhead, capital, and collections.

   c. Comparisons of the servicer's costs and revenues with industry averages.

46. Evaluate management's planning process for future servicing activities. Determine whether:

   a. Current systems are capable of handling the requirements for the current and anticipated securitization volume.

   b. The planning process for the development of operating systems has been coordinated with plans for anticipated future growth in servicing obligations.

   c. Provisions exist for complete testing and personnel training before adding systems or changing existing ones significantly.

   d. A sufficient number of experienced credit administration and workout personnel are available to meet the added demands associated with increased transaction and account volumes.

47. Determine whether the bank has contracted for an appropriate amount of errors and omissions insurance to cover the risks associated with the added transaction volumes from securitization activities.

48. Determine whether internal or external auditors review the servicing function. Determine whether they:

    a. Verify loan balances.

    b. Verify notes, mortgages, security interests, collateral, etc., with outside custodians.

    c. Review loan collection and repossession activities to determine that the servicer:

- Promptly identifies problem loans;
- Charges off loans in a timely manner;
- Follows written guidelines for extensions, renegotiations, and renewal of loans;
- Clears stale items from suspense accounts in a timely manner; and
- Accounts for servicing fees properly (by amortizing excess servicing fees, for example).

## Collections

49. Review policies and procedures for collecting delinquent loans.

    a. Determine whether collection efforts are consistent with pooling and servicing agreement guidelines.

    b. Determine whether the bank documents all attempts to collect past-due payments, including the date(s) of borrower contact, the nature of communication, and the borrower's response/comment.

    c. Evaluate methods used by management to ensure that collection procedures comply with applicable state and federal laws and regulations.

# Other Roles

## Credit Enhancement Provider

50. If the bank enhances the credit of securitized products it *originates*, ensure that:

    a. It appropriately classifies the transactions as "financings" or "sales."

    b. Accounting for this obligation does not underestimate predictable losses or overestimate the adequacy of loan loss reserves.

    c. Standards for enhancing the bank's own originations are not more liberal than standards applied to securitized products originated by others.

51. Ensure that the authority to enhance the credit of other banks' securitization programs is solely in the hands of credit personnel.

52. Determine that *all* credit enhancement exposures are analyzed during the bank's internal credit review process. At a minimum, ensure that:

    a. The accounting for this contingent obligation does not underestimate predictable loan losses or overestimate the adequacy of loan loss reserves.

    b. The limits on securitized credits that the bank enhances reflect the bank's overall exposure to the originator and packager of the securitized credits.

    c. The bank consolidates its exposure to securitized credits it enhances with exposure to the same credits held in its own loan portfolio.

53. Determine whether the bank has established exposure limits for pertinent credit criteria, such as the enhancer's exposure by customers, industry, and geography. Determine whether these exposures are incorporated into systemic exposure reports.

54. Ascertain whether the bank has the capacity to fund the support they have provided. Evaluate whether the bank considers this contingent obligation in its contingency funding plans.

55. Determine that the bank's business plan for credit enhancement addresses capital allocation and ensure that the associated costs of capital usage are incorporated into pricing and transaction decisions.

56. If credit enhancement facilities are provided for third parties, ensure that risk-based capital allocations are consistent with current guidelines set forth in 12 CFR 3 and the "Instructions for the Consolidated Reports of Condition and Income."

## Trustee

These procedures supplement those in the *Comptroller's Handbook for National Trust Examiners* and are intended only to guide examiners during the evaluation of the trustee's role in the securitization process.

57. Determine whether all indentures and contracts have been reviewed by appropriate legal counsel. Establish whether the agreements have been carefully worded to specify only services that the bank is capable of performing.

58. Review how bank management evaluates proposed customers and transactions that involve the bank as trustee. At a minimum, an evaluation should consider:

    a. The bank's capacity to perform all the tasks being requested.

    b. The financial and ethical backgrounds of the customer.

    c. The reputation and financial risks of entering into a relationship with the customer or acting as trustee for the transaction.

59. Review conflicts of interest that could arise when the bank trustee acts in an additional capacity in the securitization process. If the potential for conflicts of interest is apparent, determine whether the bank's legal

counsel has reviewed the situation and rendered an opinion on its propriety.

60.  Determine whether the audit of trust work on securitized products is adequate.

## Liquidity Enhancement Provider

61.  Review agreements in which the bank agrees to provide back-up liquidity (either as a servicer or third-party provider of liquidity enhancement), and determine whether liquidity will be provided in the event of credit problems.  Consider whether:

    a.  The bank (as liquidity provider) is required to advance for delinquent receivables.

    b.  The liquidity agreements cite credit-related contingencies that would allow the bank to withhold advances.

62.  If the bank, in agreeing to provide back-up liquidity, assumes any risk of loss that would constitute providing recourse, ensure that appropriate risk-based capital is maintained by the bank.

## Underwriter and Packager

63.  Determine whether legal counsel has been used in arriving at appropriate policies and procedures governing due diligence and disclosure to investors.

    a.  Ascertain whether the bank's policy or practices require the bank to inform customers that nonpublic information in the bank's possession may be disclosed as part of the underwriting process.  If not, determine whether legal counsel concurred with the decision not to provide the disclosure and ensure that the rationale behind it has been documented.

    b.  Determine whether the bank has procedures to disclose all material information to investors.

c.    Determine whether the bank has procedures to ensure that:

- • Publicly offered securities are registered under the Securities Act of 1933; or
- • Any reliance upon an exemption from registration (privately offered securities are exempt from such registration) is supported by the opinion of counsel.

64.  Evaluate the measures taken to limit the bank's exposure in the event that an issue the institution has agreed to underwrite cannot be sold. Review systems used to quantify underwriting risks and to establish risk limits.  Consider:

- • Funding capacity necessary to support temporary and long-term inventory positions;
- • Balance sheet compatibility;
- • Diversity of customer sales base and prospects for subsequent sale; and
- • Hedging strategies.

65.  Ascertain whether the bank is prepared to make a market for all asset-backed securities that it underwrites. Also, determine whether this question is addressed in the bank's contingency funding plan.

66.  Determine whether the bank monitors securities it has underwritten and adjusts funding plans according to noted or perceived market shifts and investor actions.

67.  Review the bank's files for current information on the asset-backed security originator, credit enhancer, and other pertinent parties.  Assess the ability of these parties to meet their obligations.

## Overall Conclusions

68.  Prepare a summary memorandum detailing the results of the asset securitization examination.  Address the following:

a. Adequacy of risk management systems, including the bank's ability to identify, measure, monitor, and control the risks of securitization.

b. Adequacy of the strategic plan or business plan for asset securitization.

c. Adequacy of policies and operating procedures and adherence thereto.

d. Quality and depth of management supervision and operating personnel.

e. Adequacy of management information systems.

f. Propriety of accounting systems and regulatory reporting.

g. Compliance with applicable laws, rulings, and regulations.

h. Adequacy of audit, compliance, and credit reviews.

I. Recommended corrective action regarding deficient policies, procedures, or practices and other concerns.

j. Commitments received from management to address concerns.

k. The impact of securitization activities on reputation risk, strategic risk, credit risk, transaction risk, liquidity risk, and compliance risk.

l. The impact of securitization activities on the bank's earnings and capital.

m. The bank's future prospects based on its finances and other considerations.

n. Other matters of significance.

69. Discuss examination findings and conclusions with the EIC. Based on

---

this discussion, set up a meeting with bank management to share findings and obtain any necessary commitments for corrective action.

70.   Write a memorandum specifically setting out what the OCC needs to do in the future to effectively supervise the asset securitization function. Include time frames, staffing, and workdays required.

71.   Update the examination work papers.

## Regulations

12 CFR 3, Minimum Capital Ratios; Issuance of Directives (including Appendix A)

## Issuances

Banking Circular 177, "Corporate Contingency Planning"
*Comptroller's Handbook* , "Capital and Dividends"
*Comptroller's Handbook* , "Mortgage Banking"
*Comptroller's Handbook for National Bank Examiners*, "Funds Management," Section 405
Consolidated Reports of Condition and Income (the Call Reports)
Financial Accounting Standard 125, "Accounting for Transfers and Servicing of Financial Assets and Extinguishments of Liabilities"
OCC 96-52, "Securitization — Guidelines for National Banks"

www.ingramcontent.com/pod-product-compliance
Lightning Source LLC
Chambersburg PA
CBHW080317290526
45790CB00005B/2079